KITCHEN GARDEN
COOKBOOK

Jeanne Kelley

PHOTOGRAPHS
Ray Kachatorian

weldon**owen**

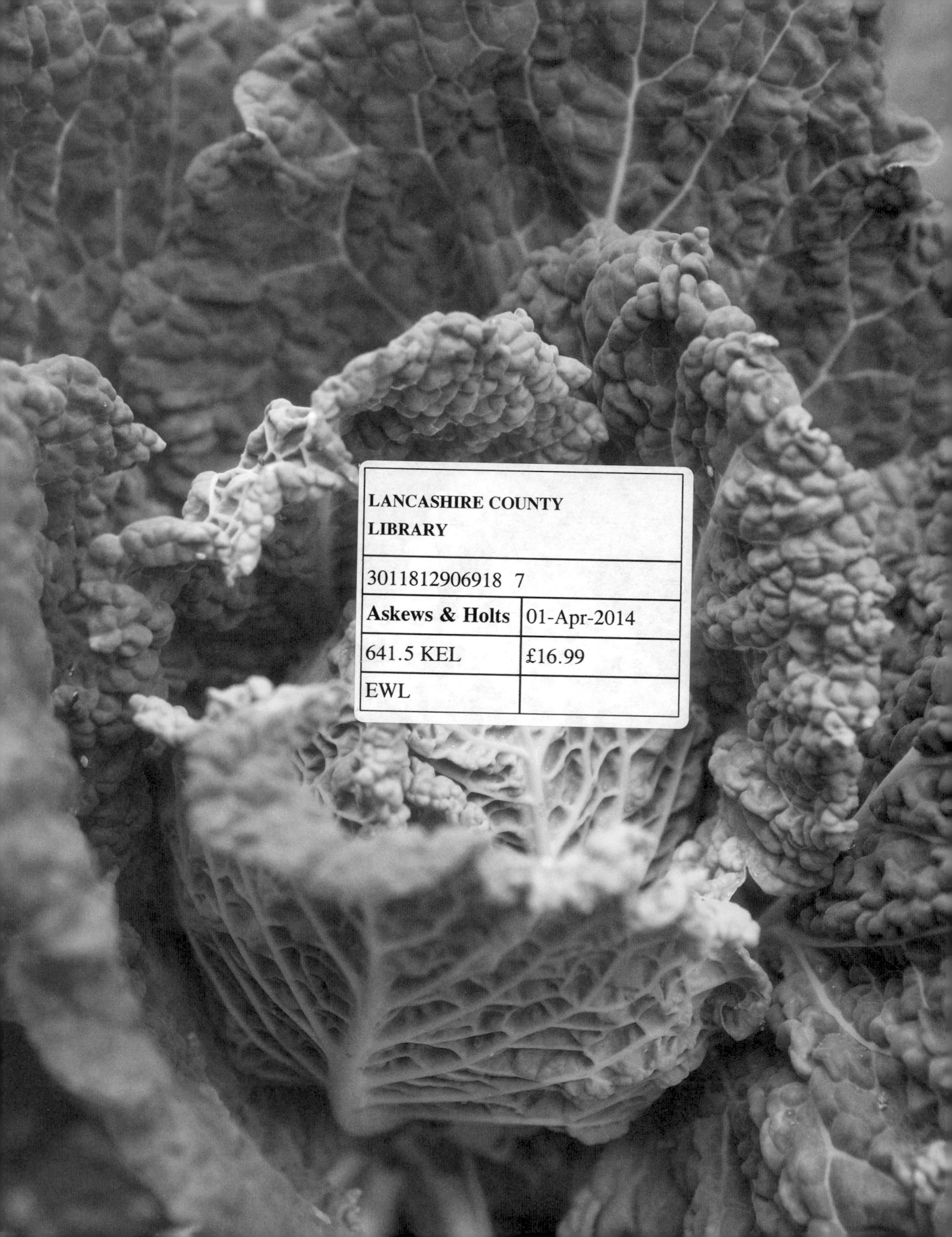

A note from Jeanne

the garden 9
Welcome to the garden

spring 15
Peas & fava beans • Spring greens
Asparagus • Radishes & green onions
Spring herbs • Strawberries

summer 73
Tomatoes • Summer vines • Snap & shell beans
Summer herbs • Berries & stone fruits

fall & winter 129
Greens • Roots & tubers • Winter squashes &
pumpkins • Winter herbs • Citrus, apples & pears

the coop & the hive 181
An introduction to chickens • Egg recipes
An introduction to bees • Honey recipes

Preparing a meal for family or friends is one of life's great pleasures. Sitting down to a table laden with great food is a delight as well—and a welcome reward for time spent in the kitchen. But nearly everyone agrees that there is joy in both cooking and eating. Can raising fruits and vegetables, and keeping chickens and honeybees, deliver that same level of happiness? The answer is most definitely yes.

Gardening is undeniably hard work. It involves lots of planning, physical labor, time, and, of course, dirt, but the payoff can be huge. I have made the necessary chores of planting, watering, feeding, and weeding part of my weekly routine, and have found that they are more than worth the joy I feel at harvesttime. To be able to pick something for dinner rather than pick up something for dinner is an unrivaled experience. Caring for my chickens and bees demands plenty of time and energy, too, but when I gather eggs from my coop or pull a honeycomb from my backyard hive, I know that all those long hours of work have been rewarded.

In the following pages you'll find a primer for planting many of the "greatest hits" of a classic backyard vegetable and fruit garden. There are tomatoes, of course, as nothing beats their sun-warmed, vine-plucked popularity. In fact, the desire to harvest homegrown heirlooms is what got me to put in my garden. Everything from asparagus, cucumbers, and lettuces to squashes, lemons, and berries soon took their place in the plot. Those first tomatoes also led me to raising chickens and keeping bees, in the same way that cooking often follows a natural progression. For example, you might begin by making salad dressing and cookies from scratch, and with knowledge accumulated and taste acquired, continue on to baking bread with wild yeast and churning ice cream. For me, baskets of yellow Brandywine tomatoes led directly to backyard eggs and honey. My hope is that you will make a similar journey.

But this book is about much more than planting a kitchen garden and raising hens and honeybees. It is also about great food and how to make it at home, even if you don't have a garden plot or a hive of busy bees. More than 100 easy-to-prepare recipes showcase the fresh, natural flavors of just-picked fruits and vegetables, farm-fresh eggs, and sweet golden honey, whether from your backyard, your local farmers' market, or your neighborhood produce store. So even if you only have space and time to grow pots of basil, oregano, and mint in a sunny window, you will find plenty of dishes here that will inspire you to both cook and garden at home.

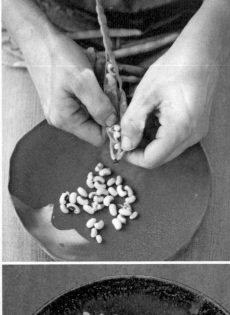

THE GARDEN

WELCOME TO THE GARDEN

If you are new to growing fruits and vegetables, just the thought of doing it can be intimidating. But once you have selected the site, dressed up the soil, and planted your first crops, nearly everything will seem easier and you'll start to take pride in your new green thumb. By harvesttime, your fears will have evaporated and your rewards will be bountiful: baskets of good-tasting, nutrient-loaded produce that you grew yourself.

selecting a site

Kitchen gardens can take many forms. If you have an open field, you can put together a small farm. If you have a modest-sized yard, raised beds are a good choice. If you have only a patio or terrace, planters, grow boxes, or other containers can provide the growing space. If you have no outdoor area, look into joining a community garden. And failing that, you can still create an herb garden on a sunny windowsill.

Wherever you decide to plant, make sure the spot gets at least six full hours of sunshine a day and has easy access to water. Plants that yield fruits like tomatoes, cucumbers, and peppers need more than six hours daily. Plants that produce edible foliage, such as lettuce, chard, and parsley, will thrive with less light.

I do most of my planting in the community garden down the street from our home. It is outfitted with raised beds of all sorts, some constructed from wooden planks, others from concrete blocks, and still others from hay bales. To locate a community garden near you, contact your city council or other local information office.

preparing the soil

Field gardens, raised-bed gardens, and container gardens all require proper soil preparation. The first step is to test the soil to determine the pH and to see how much nitrogen, phosphorous, and potassium it contains. Purchase a soil-testing kit at a garden-supply store or online. Fall is the best time to test, because if your garden patch requires tinkering, the soil will have time to mellow during the fallow winter months. Ideally, the test will show a pH level of 6.5 or 7. If the soil is too acidic, that is, the pH is too low, add limestone. If it is too alkaline, that is, the pH is too high, add sulfur, gypsum, or aluminum sulfates. For information on the proper amendments and amounts, as well as the best fertilizer to use, consult a local gardening expert or your nearest cooperative extension office.

If your garden is a farmlike plot, consider hiring someone to till the soil, or rent a rotary tiller and do it yourself. This is quite an undertaking, and chances are that if you are up to the challenge, you have probably already done quite a bit of gardening and will know the drill. The steps include sod and weed removal, tilling, amending, and then finally planting.

If you settle on raised beds, which are typically a mixture of garden soil, purchased or homemade compost, and fertilizer, use a shovel to dig down as deeply as you can and turn the soil to combine the layers. After digging, I like to use a pitchfork to mix and aerate the soil even further. This twofold dirt mixing is called double digging and is critical for the proper root structure of healthy vegetables.

The major concern when planting in a container is good drainage, both of the soil and the container itself. The soil must not be so compacted that it traps moisture and rots the roots or so loose that the water runs through quickly, leaving the roots thirsty. You can purchase potting soil or mix up your own using garden soil and amendments, keeping in mind that the soil must also be well aerated.

planting

Both plants and weather have seasons. The season for a plant begins at germination, then proceeds to growth, food production, going to seed, and dying. An annual is a plant that's entire life cycle, or season, lasts just one year. Perennials have a longer cycle, usually two or three years. In the era of year-round imported produce, it's understandable that some folks don't have a grasp of seasonal planting and eating. Unless you grow your own fruits and vegetables or shop exclusively at farmers' markets, you can become confused. Get acquainted with the plant hardiness zones drawn up by the United States Department of Agriculture, available on its website, and learn about the appropriate plants to grow each season in your climate. Don't attempt to grow vegetables out of season: summer vegetables need warm temperatures to establish and bloom; cool-weather plants will quickly go to seed without producing anything edible if exposed to too much heat.

To get maximum yield from my limited space, I practice a modified version of biointensive gardening, which combines biodynamic and French-intensive methods. It calls for raised beds, generously amended soil, and close cultivation. By putting plants right next to one another, the soil is protected from the sun, water is conserved, and the need for irrigation is minimized. No matter what planting method you choose, always use organic compost and fertilizers, both of which are available at most garden-supply stores.

watering

Water is obviously crucial to a flourishing garden. But how you water is equally important. Irrigate consistently, allowing the top few inches of the soil to become dry before applying more. Sprinkle beds gently, especially when moistening the soil around seedlings. You want the water to fall like a soft rain. I use a watering wand that screws onto the hose. It showers the soil around the vegetation until it is deeply saturated without damaging the plants. Saturation is critical, too. Check to see if the soil is moistened by digging a few inches below the surface.

growing organically

I have grown bushels of produce in my garden and have never used a pesticide. That's not to say that I haven't had to deal with a few bugs. Earwigs and pill bugs once ate through a crop of seedlings overnight. Aphids have devoured many a precious Brussels sprout, and tiny beetles occasionally like to camp out on my bed of young lettuce, making it unappealing to humans. But over the years, I've enjoyed more bug- and blemish-free fruits and vegetables than I've suffered insects. To help keep such pests at bay, maintain a tidy garden. Piles of old wood, stacks of unused pots, and unkempt shrubs provide bugs with a comfortable place to hang out. You'll decrease the pest population just by cleaning up.

Water plants properly and trim off dead leaves regularly. Weak, suffering plants are more susceptible to infestation. Harvest fruits and vegetables as they ripen so that they don't rot and attract bugs. Certain plants help with pest control too. In summer, I plant marigolds along the edge of the raised bed to attract slugs and earwigs. A few weeks into the growing season, the marigolds are usually dead, but that's okay. I'd rather grow tomatoes than marigolds. I also plant mint, which attracts good pest-eating wasps and deters bad bugs, such as cabbage worms and aphids.

a note on chickens and bees

The chickens in our backyard lay delicious eggs. Their manure composts into a rich soil amendment that helps our vegetables grow. The bees we keep make sweet honey and they pollinate the garden, ensuring it will thrive. The hens eat the bugs that would like to eat our crops, and we feed the hens tasty green scraps from the yard. The synthesis of man-hours and nature comes together in a delightful backyard meal—joyful and pretty darned amazing.

COMPOSTING

Making compost is both easy to do and a boon to your garden's productivity. A good basic "recipe" combines fruit and vegetable scraps with leaves, grass, weeds, and other garden trimmings. I give our chickens all the "good" stuff, such as apple cores and peels, and put the compostable material they don't eat, like coffee grounds, onion trimmings, and eggshells, in our compost pile. I also add chicken manure to the pile to get things cooking. Never add meat or fish scraps, bones, or diseased plants to the blend. The compost needs to be mixed regularly—a shovel is perfect for this chore—and it's always a kick to see the steam rise.

SPRING

peas oregon giant • **fava beans** windsor • **arugula** italian, wild
radicchio catalogna, red bib, chrystal hat • **spinach** catalina,
oriental giant, bloomsdale, summer perfection • **watercress**
asparagus mary washington, jersey giant, purple passion
radishes french breakfast, rainbow, easter egg II • **green onions**
evergreen hardy white, ishikura improved, white lisbon • **chives**
fennel florence, smokey • **parsley** dark green italian, moss curled,
single italian • **sorrel** common, french • **strawberries** alpine,
albion, ozark beauty, tristar, sequoia

SPRING

Spring is the busiest season in the garden for both plants and gardeners. It's a period for cleaning, planting, and growing. In warm and cool zones, it's time to get the most out of the earth and sun by enjoying a harvest of peas, radishes, green onions, asparagus, spinach, strawberries, and more and by getting summer vegetables in the ground. It's also when a crock of just-made strawberry jam sits on the breakfast table, tender spears of asparagus sizzle on the grill, and dinners are graced with lush salads of arugula, radicchio, and watercress.

For gardeners everywhere, spring is a season of renewal, when the slow, dark days of winter are over and a new garden year has formally begun. Good timing is important. You must judge when the danger of frost has passed so that you can sow seeds or plant seedlings, and you need to get your tomato plants in when it's neither too cool nor too hot to help them flourish come summer. Don't be shy about seeking the advice of a local expert—at the nursery, at the farmers' market, at the garden club, or from the best gardener in your neighborhood—to learn when to act to ensure your spring and summer gardens thrive.

getting ready

When it warms up enough to be outdoors, it's time to start your garden cleanup. Before you can plant, you need to survey the condition of your raised beds or planters, then rebuild vegetable beds if necessary before amending and prepping the soil. Also, take a look at any trees and shrubs that surround your beds and trim them before they put on too much new growth that threatens to shade your garden. Remove any mulch that has protected overwintering plants and pull all weeds from the moist ground.

what to do in colder climates

Spring can be a frustrating time for gardeners who live where it snows. Just when the almanac predicts the last frost, a cold front often appears on the Doppler, making it impossible to get any seeds in the ground. If this happens, consider starting seeds indoors or planting nursery starts to get a jump on the growing season. When planting seeds indoors, select a sunny spot, preferably near a south-facing window. Fill small pots that have good drainage with potting soil. Once the seeds are planted, water them carefully. You want the soil to be moist yet not wet; a spray bottle works well for this job. When the weather warms enough for outdoor planting, harden off your established seedlings—that is, acclimate them to the outdoors before transplanting them—by first exposing them to some cool shade during the day and then eventually letting them spend the night outside.

Friends of mine who live in a real-winter climate take advantage of early spring by planting quick-grow (or early-harvest) vegetables like radishes, green onions, and peas. The growing season for these vegetables is short enough that they can go from seed to harvest with plenty of time left over to ready the bed for the next succession of planting for summer.

what to do in warmer climates

Gardeners in warmer zones plant spring favorites in the fall so that they can harvest and re-plant in early spring. It may seem odd that the early-harvest vegetables of spring are planted before winter even starts, but cool weather, shorter days, and fewer sunny hours cause the plants to mature very slowly. Spring vegetables planted in spring often fail to thrive because an abundance of heat and sun can cause them to go to seed.

Come spring, peas and fava beans are popular in my garden and at my table. I like to pair sweet, delicate peas with fresh ricotta atop bruschetta or with watercress in soup, or lime-green favas with seared cheese and green onions. Recruit your children to help you shell peas and favas. It is a great way to pique their interest in eating vegetables.

how to grow peas & fava beans

select peas

Two main categories of peas are grown: edible pod peas that you eat pod and all, and peas that you shell. The two best-known edible pod peas are flat, broad snow peas, sometimes called Chinese peas, and sugar snap peas. Be sure to select stringless varieties for planting to save time in the kitchen. Although most sugar snaps are best when the peas are plump but still small, Oregon Giants, with their big, sweet, crunchy peas and thick, succulent pods, are my favorite sugar snap.

The English, or garden, pea is the most common type of shelling pea. If you have never eaten fresh-from-the garden English peas, you are in for a treat when you shell your first crop. They are less starchy and dramatically more flavorful than their store-bought (fresh or frozen) cousins.

plant and maintain peas

Pea seeds are good sized, and when the sprouts emerge, they are large and unmistakably peas. In cooler climates, plant seeds as soon as the ground can be worked. Sow them about 1 inch (2.5 cm) deep and 4 inches (10 cm) apart in rich, good-draining, sandy soil in full or partial sun. In warmer areas, plant them in the fall. Peas are climbers, which means they need a trellis or some other sort of support. I use the same cages for peas in the fall that I use for tomatoes in the summer. Keep the soil moist but not saturated. Seeds bred for late and early harvests are available, and it's a good idea to plant both types so that you aren't harvesting your crop all at once. Alternatively, you can stagger plantings a week or so apart. I plant 8 to 12 seeds around one or two cages, wait a week, and then plant more seeds around more cages. Frequent harvesting encourages more growth. Most pods are ready to harvest when they are 2 to 3 inches (5 to 7.5 cm) long.

plant and maintain fava beans

The fava plant, with its pale green leaves and pretty white-and-black flowers, is a handsome addition to the garden. The large, leathery pods, 6 to 8 inches (15 to 20 cm) long, grow out of the plant's *Jack-and-the-Beanstalk*-like central stalk. Each pod contains 4 to 6 big flat beans.

Although favas are not as easy to grow as peas, they are relatively undemanding. They thrive in rich, well-draining soil and like cool temperatures but lots of bright sunlight. Sow seeds 1 inch (2.5 cm) deep and 4 inches (10 cm) apart in rows 18 inches (45 cm) apart. Keep the soil around the plants weed-free and moist, but don't overwater. Aphids like fava beans, so use an insecticidal soap if your plants get infested. The pods will be ready to harvest in 75 to 90 days.

ricotta & pea crostini with tarragon & pink peppercorns

extra-virgin olive oil, 2 tbsp, plus more for brushing

green onion, 1, sliced

green garlic, 1 tbsp sliced or 1 clove garlic, chopped

English peas, 1½ cups (7½ oz/235 g) shelled

fresh tarragon leaves, 1½ tbsp minced, plus whole leaves for garnish

kosher salt and freshly ground pepper

ricotta cheese, ¾ cup (6 oz/185)

Parmesan cheese, ½ cup (2 oz/60 g) grated

baguette, 24 thin slices

pink peppercorns, for garnish

This delicately flavored and out-of-the ordinary appetizer is a welcome addition to any of my spring dinners or cocktail parties. I like the flavor of whole-grain bread, but a traditional French baguette works nicely as well.

Preheat the oven to 400°F (200°C). In a heavy frying pan over medium heat, warm the 2 tbsp olive oil. Add the green onion and green garlic and sauté until tender, about 1 minute. Add the peas and tarragon and stir to coat. Add ⅓ cup (3 fl oz/80 ml) water and a sprinkle of salt and cook until the peas are tender and almost all of the water has evaporated, about 7 minutes. Remove from the heat and let cool slightly.

Transfer to a food processor, add the ricotta and Parmesan, and process until smooth. Season with salt and pepper. (The mixture can be covered and refrigerated for up to 2 days before continuing.)

Arrange the baguette slices on a large rimmed baking sheet. Brush the slices lightly with olive oil. Place in the oven until lightly toasted, about 8 minutes.

Spread the toasts thickly with the purée and return to the baking sheet. Return to the oven and heat just until the purée is warmed through, about 7 minutes.

Arrange the crostini on a platter, sprinkle with some peppercorns and tarragon leaves, and serve.

pan-seared halloumi with fava beans, mint & lemon

Preparing fava beans can be a bit of a chore, but it's definitely worth it. The pods come off easily, but even though the clear, thin skin that encases each bean is edible, on more mature beans it can be tough and bitter and will also need to be removed. When harvested very small—about the size of your small finger—the entire bean can be eaten, pod and all.

Bring a small saucepan filled with salted water to a boil. Add the fava beans and boil until the skins begin to blister, about 2 minutes. Drain the beans, let cool until they can be handled, and then slip off the skins. (The fava beans can be prepared up to 1 day in advance, covered, and refrigerated.)

In a small bowl, whisk together 2 tbsp of the olive oil, the lemon juice, and ¼ tsp of the lemon zest. Season with salt and set aside.

In a heavy frying pan over medium heat, warm 1 tbsp oil. Add the green onions and garlic and sauté until tender, about 1 minute. Add the fava beans and mint and stir until coated. Add ¼ cup (2 fl oz/60 ml) water, cover, and cook until the fava beans are tender, about 4 minutes. Uncover, reduce the heat to the lowest possible setting to keep the beans warm, and season with salt.

While the fava beans are cooking, sprinkle the cheese slices on both sides with the remaining ½ tsp lemon zest and the red pepper flakes. In a large nonstick frying pan, warm the remaining 1 tbsp oil over medium heat. Add the cheese and cook, turning once, until golden brown on both sides, about 4 minutes.

Spoon the fava beans onto a serving platter and arrange the cheese slices on top. Whisk the vinaigrette briefly to recombine, then spoon over the cheese. Garnish with mint leaves and lemon wedges and serve.

kosher salt

fava beans, 1½ lb (750 g), shelled

extra-virgin olive oil, 4 tbsp

fresh lemon juice, 1 tbsp

lemon zest, ¾ tsp grated

green onions, ⅓ cup (1 oz/30 g) sliced

garlic, 2 cloves, minced

fresh mint leaves, ⅓ cup (⅓ oz/10 g), plus more for garnish

halloumi cheese, about ½ lb (250 g), cut into 8 slices

red pepper flakes, about ¼ tsp

lemon wedges, for serving

three peas with barley, chile & green garlic

kosher salt

sugar snap peas, 6 oz (185 g), trimmed

English peas, 1 cup (5 oz/155 g) shelled

pearl barley, ½ cup (3½ oz/105 g)

rice vinegar, 2 tbsp

soy sauce, 2 tbsp

golden brown sugar, 1 tbsp firmly packed

sambal oelek or other pure chile paste, 1 tsp

Asian sesame oil, 1 tbsp

green garlic, ¼ cup (¾ oz/20 g) thinly sliced, or 4 cloves garlic, minced

green onions, ¼ cup (¾ oz/20 g) sliced

fresh kaffir lime leaves, 2

pea shoots, about ¼ lb (125 g)

MAKES 4 SERVINGS

Pea shoots are the young, tender tips and vines of the snow pea or the sugar snap pea plant. Once your plants are established and producing an abundance of pods, clip off leaf and tendril sections about 4 inches (10 cm) long. If you don't have your own plants, look for these tender shoots at farmers' markets or Asian grocery stores. Sambal oelek (or *ulek*) is an Indonesian chile paste, and tart, citrusy kaffir lime leaves are used in Southeast Asian cooking. Look for both products in Asian markets.

Bring a large saucepan half full of salted water to a boil over high heat. Add the snap peas and peas and cook until tender-crisp, about 1 minute. Using a slotted spoon, transfer the vegetables to a colander and rinse under cold water. Set aside. Return the saucepan to a boil, add the barley and cook until tender, about 45 minutes. Drain and set aside.

In a small bowl, whisk together the rice vinegar, soy sauce, 2 tbsp water, brown sugar, and sambal oelek until blended. In a large, heavy frying pan over high heat, warm the sesame oil. Add the green garlic, green onions, and lime leaves and stir-fry until the green onions are tender, about 30 seconds. Add the reserved snap peas, peas, and barley along with the pea shoots, and stir to coat. Pour in the soy sauce mixture and stir and toss until the peas and pea shoots are tender and the liquid is absorbed, about 4 minutes. Transfer to a warmed serving dish and serve.

english pea & watercress soup

extra-virgin olive oil, 1 tbsp

green onions, ⅔ cup (2 oz/60 g) sliced, plus more for garnish

garlic, 2 cloves, chopped

fresh ginger, 1 tsp peeled and grated

chicken broth, 5 cups (40 fl oz/1.25 l)

russet potato, 1 (about ½ lb/250 g), peeled and cut into 1-inch (2.5-cm) chunks

watercress, 4 cups (4 oz/125 g), leaves and tender stems only

English peas, 3 cups (15 oz/470 g) shelled

crème fraîche, ⅓ cup (3 oz/90 g), plus more for garnish

kosher salt and freshly ground pepper

MAKES 4–6 SERVINGS

Emerald green and rich with such spring favorites as peas, watercress, and green onions, this soup is the perfect starter for an Easter lunch or St. Patrick's Day supper. I sneak a russet potato into the mix, giving the soup a silky, smooth texture without weighing it down with lots of cream.

In a large, heavy saucepan over medium-high heat, warm the olive oil. Add the green onions, garlic, and ginger and sauté until the green onions are tender, about 1 minute. Add the broth and potato and bring to a simmer. Reduce the heat to medium, cover, and cook until the potato is very tender, about 12 minutes. Stir in the watercress and peas, re-cover, and continue to cook until the peas are tender, about 4 minutes. Remove from the heat and let cool slightly.

Working in batches, transfer the soup to a blender and process until smooth. Return the soup to the saucepan and whisk in the crème fraîche. (The soup can be cooled, covered, and refrigerated for up to 3 days.)

Return the pan to medium heat and reheat just until the soup reaches a simmer. Season with salt and pepper. Ladle the soup into warmed bowls, garnish with crème fraîche and green onions, and serve.

seared scallops with snow peas & green garlic

grapeseed oil, 1½ tbsp

large sea scallops, 10 oz (315 g)

kosher salt and freshly ground pepper

unsalted butter, 1 tbsp

green garlic, 2 tbsp thinly sliced

green onions, ¼ cup (¾ oz/20 g) sliced

snow peas, 6 oz (185 g), trimmed

dry white wine, ¼ cup (2 fl oz/60 ml)

honey, 1 tsp

The best way to cook scallops is to sear them in a superhot frying pan. The outsides become nicely browned and crisped and the insides stay tender and moist. Snow peas also stay wonderfully crisp when cooked briefly in a hot pan. This is the first dish that I make when my snow peas yield more than just a sweet, crunchy snack while gardening.

In a heavy frying pan over high heat, warm the grapeseed oil. When the oil is hot, season the scallops on both sides with salt and pepper and add to the pan. Sear the scallops, turning once, until well browned on both sides and just barely cooked in the center, about 3 minutes. Transfer the scallops to a plate.

Reduce the heat to medium-high and add half of the butter to the pan. Add the green garlic and green onions and sauté until tender, about 30 seconds. Add the snow peas and stir and toss until tender-crisp, about 2 minutes. Divide the snow peas between 2 warmed plates.

Pour the wine into the pan and bring to a boil, stirring to dislodge any browned bits from the pan bottom. Whisk in the honey and the remaining butter and season with salt and pepper.

Arrange the scallops on top of the peas, and pour the pan sauce over the top, dividing it evenly. Serve.

My spring garden is thick with all kinds of greens, from peppery arugula and mildly bitter radicchio to delicate watercress and emerald green spinach. They give my backyard a lush appearance and my dinner table a wide range of flavors and textures. I clip them throughout the season for adding to salads and sautés, sandwiches and pizzas.

how to grow spring greens

plant and maintain arugula

I live in a temperate climate zone, so I am usually successful growing arugula year-round, though springtime is when this Mediterranean annual shines. I plant an Italian variety with leaves as big and showy as those on a romaine head. In fact, they are so big that some people don't even believe they are arugula, until the spiciness hits their palate.

In colder climates, plant seeds in rich, well-draining soil in full sun after the threat of frost is over, then thin seedlings to 6 inches (15 cm) apart. In warmer climates, sow seeds the same way, but in partial shade. The seeds germinate quickly, and you can sometimes pick tender baby leaves just a month after planting. Clip off blossoms as they appear to keep plants producing. I harvest the outer leaves near the base; new leaves will emerge at the center. Some gardeners pull up whole plants, and then sow more seeds every few weeks.

plant and maintain radicchio

Part of the hardy chicory clan, radicchio counts Belgian endive, curly endive, and escarole among its kin. I grow burgundy-leaved radicchio, sowing seeds in late winter in well-amended soil for a spring harvest (or in late summer for a fall to winter harvest). Sow seeds no more than ¼ inch (6 mm) deep, then thin seedlings to 8 inches (20 cm) apart. Open-leaf varieties fare better in warmer zones and the tight-headed types are more successful where it's cool. To harvest, cut the plant cleanly at ground level.

plant and maintain spinach

Oriental Giant, with its huge, succulent, pointy leaves, is my favorite spinach variety. People see it and often joke that it's spinach on steroids. You can start any variety from seed, indoors or directly in the garden, as soon as the soil can be worked. If you start the seeds indoors, the seedlings can be difficult to transplant because of their shallow roots, so I usually plant nursery starts directly in the garden, spacing them 6 inches (15 cm) apart. Plants started from seed will be ready to pick in 4 to 6 weeks. To harvest, clip just the outer leaves or the whole plant. Spinach gets bitter once it bolts, so if you live where spring can be hot, plant in partial shade.

plant and maintain **watercress**

I walk my dog in an arroyo where watercress flourishes, and I would harvest pretty fronds from the creek if I didn't know that runoff from a huge municipal golf course fed the water that feeds the watercress. As the name implies, watercress is a cress—a leafy vegetable—that grows in water, and I highly recommend that you forage it from clean brooks and ponds, if possible. You can also sow seeds of a land variety in early spring in moist soil. Finally, you can grow watercress hydroponically. The easiest way to do this is to purchase a bunch at the market, put it in a bucket of water, and change the water daily (you can use it to water the rest of your garden). The stems will send out shoots that will eventually leaf out and multiply. Harvest the watercress by topping them, leaving about 3 inches (7.5 cm) of stem at the base to grow back.

marinated flank steak with lemony arugula & feta salad

Ground sumac—a deep red spice available at Middle Eastern markets—cumin, and feta give this flavorful, grilled steak exotic zip, and the tart, fresh salad makes for a lovely garnish and bright counterpoint to the beef. I frequently serve this to dinner guests as it's a real crowd-pleaser.

In a small bowl, whisk together the olive oil, lemon juice, garlic, cumin, and sumac. Place the steak on a plate. Spoon half of the dressing over both sides of the steak, then sprinkle both sides with salt and pepper. Let stand at room temperature for 15 minutes (or cover and refrigerate overnight).

Prepare a medium fire for direct-heat cooking in a charcoal or gas grill. Arrange the steak on the grill rack directly over the fire and grill, turning once, until seared on both sides and medium-rare inside, about 8 minutes.

Transfer the steak to a cutting board and let rest for at least 5 minutes. In a bowl, combine the arugula, green onion, parsley, and feta and drizzle the remaining dressing over the top. Season with salt and pepper and toss together well. Slice the steak, arrange the slices on a platter, top with the arugula salad, and serve.

extra-virgin olive oil, 2 tbsp

fresh lemon juice, 2 tbsp

garlic, 2 cloves, pressed

ground cumin, 2 tsp

ground sumac, 2 tsp

flank steak, 1 lb (250 g)

kosher salt and freshly ground pepper

arugula leaves, 2 cups (2 oz/60 g)

green onions, 2, thinly sliced

fresh flat-leaf parsley leaves, 2 tbsp

feta cheese, ½ cup (2 oz/60 g) crumbled

mixed spring greens with chive vinaigrette

Snipped chives and just-picked greens make for a cool green-on-green salad. Use any combination of greens that you have in the garden or kitchen. I often enjoy this spring treat with a hard-boiled egg and slice of buttered country toast.

In a salad bowl, using the back of a wooden spoon, muddle the chives and ¼ tsp salt until bright green. Whisk in the vinegar, then the olive oil. Add the greens and toss gently until the greens are lightly coated. Season with pepper and serve.

fresh chives, 2 tbsp snipped

kosher salt and freshly ground pepper

white wine vinegar, 2 tsp

extra-virgin olive oil, 1½ tbsp

mixed greens such as arugula, watercress, and spinach, 8 cups (8 oz/250 g)

orzo, radicchio & arugula salad

kosher salt and freshly ground pepper

orzo, 1½ cups (10½ oz/330 g)

extra-virgin olive oil, ¼ cup (2 fl oz/60 ml)

garlic, 2 cloves, pressed

balsamic vinegar, ¼ cup (2 fl oz/60 ml)

green onions, ½ cup thinly sliced

baby arugula leaves, 1 cup (1 oz/30 g)

radicchio or other red chicory, 1 cup (3 oz/90 g) thinly sliced

Parmesan cheese, ½ cup (2 oz/60 g) grated

pine nuts, ½ cup (2½ oz/75 g), toasted

fresh flat-leaf parsley leaves, ¼ cup (¼ oz/7 g)

MAKES 6 SERVINGS

I like to serve this salad with grilled sausages for dinner or just on its own for lunch. It transports well, too, which makes it a good choice for picnics, potlucks, and lunch boxes.

Bring a pot of water to a rapid boil and season generously with salt. Add the orzo, stir well, and cook until al dente, 7–9 minutes or according to package directions. Drain the orzo and transfer to a large bowl. (Do not rinse the orzo.)

Immediately stir in the olive oil and garlic and let stand until cool. Stir in the vinegar, then the green onions, arugula, radicchio, Parmesan, pine nuts, and parsley, distributing the ingredients evenly. Season with salt and pepper and serve.

sautéed spinach with a splash of cream

unsalted butter, 1 tbsp

green onion, 1, sliced

garlic, 1 clove, minced

spinach leaves, 10 cups (10 oz/315 g)

heavy cream, 2 tbsp

MAKES 2 SERVINGS

Creamed spinach is an old-fashioned favorite, but fresh spinach doesn't need the thick, heavy white sauce that binds and dulls the greens in most recipes. This light take on the classic showcases the quality of freshly harvested leaves.

In a large, deep frying pan over medium-high heat, melt the butter. Add the green onion and garlic and sauté until tender, about 30 seconds. Add the spinach and sauté until tender and wilted, about 2 minutes. Pour the cream over the spinach and toss just until the spinach is well coated, about 30 seconds. Transfer to a warmed serving bowl and serve.

pancetta, radicchio & red onion pizza

Sweet red onions, nutty fontina, salty pancetta, and mildly bitter radicchio combine sublimely on this grown-up pizza. I usually double the recipe for the dough so I can either make a simpler pie for the kids or just because two pizzas are better than one! Serve it as an appetizer, cut into small pieces, or as a main course.

In a large, heavy frying pan over medium heat, cook the pancetta, stirring occasionally, until it is almost crisp, about 3 minutes. Transfer the pancetta to a plate. Add the onion to the pan and sauté until tender, about 8 minutes. Remove from the heat.

Position a rack in the upper third of the oven and a second rack in the lower third of the oven and preheat to 400°F (200°C). Sprinkle a large, heavy rimmed baking sheet with the cornmeal.

On a lightly floured work surface, roll out the dough in a rectangle measuring about 11 by 13 inches (28 by 33 cm). Transfer the dough to the prepared baking sheet and brush the top surface with olive oil. Spread the garlic over the dough, then sprinkle evenly with the fontina, onions, and radicchio. Sprinkle the pancetta, Parmesan, and red pepper flakes evenly over the top, then season with salt.

Place the baking sheet on the bottom rack of the oven and bake until the bottom of the pizza is golden brown (lift the edge with a spatula to check), about 15 minutes. Transfer the pizza to the top rack and bake until the top is golden, about 5 minutes longer. Transfer to a cutting board and sprinkle with the parsley. Cut into pieces and serve.

pancetta, 3 oz (90 g) thinly sliced, cut into 1-inch (2.5-cm) pieces

red onions, 2, thinly sliced

cornmeal, about 1 tbsp

pizza dough (page 215), about ¾ lb (340 g)

extra-virgin olive oil, for brushing

garlic, 2 cloves, pressed

fontina or whole-milk mozzarella cheese, 1¾ cups (7 oz/220 g) shredded

radicchio or other red chicory, 1½ cups (4½ oz/140 g) thinly sliced

Parmesan cheese, ½ cup (2 oz/60 g) grated

red pepper flakes, ¼ tsp

kosher salt

fresh flat-leaf parsley leaves, 2 tbsp chopped

Growing asparagus requires patience and commitment: patience because you will have to wait three years before the first decent harvest, and commitment because the plants can live up to fifteen years. But once planted, this spring favorite requires little attention from the gardener and will shine in the kitchen, whether tossed with pasta, paired with couscous, or deliciously smoky and charred from the grill.

how to grow asparagus

plant and maintain asparagus

Select a sunny, out-of-the-way place to devote to your "patch" of this long-living perennial. A planter along a fence is a good spot. Asparagus, like strawberries, is most commonly grown from crowns. (You can sow seeds, but they take from 3 to 6 weeks to germinate indoors before you transplant them to their outdoor home.) Purchase crowns when they become available from your local nursery or an online source, usually in early spring. Once established, each crown will produce about ¾ pound (375 g) of spears a year. Martha Washington is a common disease-resistant variety with a high yield.

Approximately 1 month before the last predicted frost, plant the crowns about 5 inches (13 cm) deep and 12 to 18 inches (30 to 45 cm) apart in rich soil with good drainage. (In warmer zones, crowns can be planted in fall.) The asparagus will send up shoots in spring and into summer, but don't do any harvesting the first year. Allow the spears to grow tall and fern out, and then die back in the fall, keeping the bed well weeded at all times. This undisturbed cycle allows for the plants to become established and spread underground. Keep asparagus watered and fertilized throughout the summer and fall. The second year, you will be able to enjoy a few spears, but you won't have a significant yield until the third or fourth year.

harvest asparagus

Choose spears that are at least as stocky as a pencil. To harvest, cut off the spears at a 90-degree angle just above the ground, taking care to not to damage new growth.

Larger than traditional couscous, Israeli couscous is a pearl-shaped, toasted semolina product. I like to serve this hot as a side dish to garlicky lamb chops. Any leftovers taste good cold or at room temperature the next day.

In a heavy saucepan over medium heat, warm 1 tbsp of the olive oil. Add the couscous and sauté until golden brown, about 5 minutes. Add 1¾ cups (14 fl oz/430 ml) water, cover, and simmer until the liquid is absorbed and the couscous is tender, about 10 minutes.

In a large, heavy frying pan over high heat, warm 1 tbsp of the olive oil. When the oil is hot, add the asparagus and garlic and sprinkle with salt, then sauté until the asparagus is tender-crisp, about 3 minutes. Transfer the asparagus to a serving bowl and stir in the couscous. In a small bowl, whisk together the remaining 2 tbsp olive oil, the lemon zest, and the juice. Add to the couscous and asparagus along with the green onions and Parmesan and toss to combine. Season with salt and pepper and serve.

warm asparagus & israeli couscous salad

extra-virgin olive oil, 4 tbsp (2 fl oz/60 ml)

Israeli couscous, 1⅓ cups (6 oz/170 g)

thin asparagus spears, 2 lb (1 kg), trimmed and sliced into 1-inch (2.5-cm) pieces

garlic, 2 cloves, minced

kosher salt and freshly ground pepper

lemon zest, ½ tsp grated

fresh lemon juice, 2 tbsp

green onions, ½ cup (1½ oz/45 g) sliced

Parmesan cheese, ⅓ cup (1½ oz/45 g) grated

MAKES 2 SERVINGS

In a large nonstick frying pan over medium-high heat, warm the olive oil. Add the asparagus and stir and toss constantly until lightly coated with the oil, about 1 minute. Add 2 tbsp water, cover, and cook until the water evaporates and the asparagus is just tender, about 2 minutes.

Reduce the heat to medium and shake the pan to distribute the asparagus evenly over the bottom. Pour the eggs over the asparagus, being careful not to dislodge the asparagus, and season with salt and pepper. Cook until the eggs are just set on the bottom, about 3 minutes.

Sprinkle the omelet evenly with the cheese and chives. Cover the pan and remove from the heat. Let stand until the eggs are just set and the cheese is heated through, about 3 minutes. Slide the omelet onto a large, flat platter. Serve warm or at room temperature.

goat cheese, asparagus & chive omelet

extra-virgin olive oil, 1 tbsp

thin asparagus spears, 10 oz (315 g), trimmed and sliced on the diagonal into 3-inch (7.5-cm) pieces

large eggs, 4, lightly beaten

kosher salt and freshly ground pepper

fresh goat cheese, 2 oz (60 g), crumbled

fresh chives, 2 tbsp snipped

pappardelle with asparagus & cream

kosher salt and freshly ground pepper

dried pappardelle, ¼ lb (125 g)

thin asparagus spears, ½ lb (250 g), trimmed and sliced on the diagonal into 2½-inch (6-cm) pieces

heavy cream, ⅓ cup (3 fl oz/80 ml)

dry white wine, 1 tbsp

garlic, 1 clove, pressed

lemon zest, ½ tsp grated

green onions, ¼ cup (¾ oz/20 g), thinly sliced

Parmesan cheese, ¼ cup (1 oz/30 g) grated, plus more for serving

fresh flat-leaf parsley leaves, 2 tbsp chopped

MAKES 2 SERVINGS

This elegant pasta can be part of a spring celebration dinner. Start with Herbed Cheese and Radish Crostini (page 51), follow with English Pea and Watercress Soup (page 28), serve the pasta as your main course, and finish with Strawberries with Honey and Lavender (page 68).

Bring a pot of water to a rapid boil and salt generously. Add the pasta, stir well, and cook until about 2 minutes shy of al dente, about 8 minutes or according to package directions. Add the asparagus and boil until the asparagus is tender and the pasta is al dente, about 2 minutes longer.

Meanwhile, in a small saucepan over medium-high heat, combine the cream, wine, garlic, and lemon zest and bring to a full boil. Reduce the heat to medium and simmer until lightly thickened, about 30 seconds.

Drain the pasta and asparagus and transfer to a warmed serving bowl. Add the cream mixture, green onions, Parmesan cheese, and parsley and toss to coat the pasta evenly. Season with salt and pepper and serve, passing additional cheese at the table.

Early spring at my farmers' market offers asparagus and blushing grapefruit that are so fresh and enticing, they are perfect in a vibrant salad such as this, with smoked salmon and tender arugula from the garden.

Pour the grapefruit juice into a bowl. Whisk the vinegar and green onion into the juice, then whisk in the olive oil. Season with salt and pepper. Set the dressing aside.

Pour water to a depth of 1 inch (2.5 cm) into a large frying pan and season with salt. Bring the water to a boil over high heat. Add the asparagus, cover, reduce the heat to medium, and simmer until the asparagus is tender-crisp, about 2 minutes. Drain the asparagus then plunge into ice water. Drain well.

Arrange the asparagus, grapefruit sections, arugula leaves, and salmon on a large serving platter, drizzle with the dressing, and serve.

smoked salmon, asparagus & grapefruit salad

pink or ruby grapefruit, 1 large, cut into segments (page 217), juices reserved

white balsamic vinegar, 1 tbsp

green onion, 1 tbsp minced

extra-virgin olive oil, 2 tbsp

kosher salt and freshly ground pepper

thin asparagus spears, 1 lb (500 g), trimmed

arugula leaves, 4 cups (4 oz/125 g)

smoked salmon, ¼ lb (125 g), sliced into strips 1 inch (2.5 cm) wide

I have a niece who arrives each spring bearing bunches of wild asparagus harvested along the gravel road that leads to her ranch. This is the dish we make to celebrate her visit and to mark the arrival of spring.

Prepare a medium fire for direct-heat cooking in a charcoal or gas grill. Spread the asparagus on a large rimmed baking sheet. Drizzle with the olive oil, sprinkle with the lemon zest, and season with salt and pepper, then toss to coat. Arrange the asparagus on the grill rack directly over the fire and grill, turning occasionally, until crisp-tender, about 2 minutes.

Transfer the asparagus to a platter. Garnish with the chives and parsley and serve, passing the mayonnaise at the table.

grilled asparagus with lemon-herb mayonnaise

medium asparagus spears, 1½ lb (750 g), trimmed

extra-virgin olive oil, 1½ tbsp

lemon zest, 1 tsp grated

kosher salt and freshly ground pepper

fresh chives, 2 tbsp snipped

fresh flat-leaf parsley leaves, 2 tbsp

lemon-herb mayonnaise (page 216)

Radishes and green onions are "quick-grow" crops. You can plant them in colder climates just after the danger of frost has passed and they'll be ready for harvest in time to replant the bed with "summer" vegetables. Green onions are delicious grilled, radishes deliver a nice crunch to crostini and slaw, and both vegetables are at home in salads and sandwiches.

how to grow
radishes & green onions

plant and maintain radishes

Adults like to plant radishes because they are easy to grow, and kids like them because pulling them up is such fun. And if you grow one of the mild French Breakfast varieties, the kids will enjoy eating them too. In cold climates, plant radishes as soon as the ground can be worked; in warmer areas, plant them in late winter and early spring. Sow the seeds about ½ inch (12 mm) deep and 1 inch (2.5 cm) apart in well-worked soil. When the leaves on the sprouts are about 2 inches (5 cm) tall, thin the seedlings to at least 2 inches (5 cm) apart—the bulbs need sufficient room to develop—and save the thinned sprouts for a tasty salad. Water and weed regularly for nicely shaped bulbs too.

harvest radishes

Your radishes will be ready to harvest in 25 to 30 days, depending on variety. Don't allow them to grow too large or they will be unpleasantly peppery and woody.

plant and maintain green onions

Also known as scallions or bunching onions, green onions are either white onions that are harvested before the bulb is mature or cultivars that have been developed specifically to yield green onions. I plant cultivars—Evergreen Hardy White, White Lisbon, and Ishikura Improved are good choices—which generally grow faster than regular onions and can be cultivated from seeds or "sets." The latter, which are like small, tight bunches, can be purchased at most nurseries. I recommend growing green onions from sets, especially if you plan to grow and harvest them in early spring before replanting the bed for summer.

To plant onion sets, separate the bunches into individual onions, being careful not to damage the root end. Pick off any spent or withered pieces. Select a spot with full sun and rich soil, and space the onions 2 to 3 inches (5 to 7.5 cm) apart, inserting each bulb so it is just covered with dirt and lightly pinching the soil around the bulb so the onion stands upright. Keep the ground slightly moist throughout the growing season.

harvest green onions

Harvest the onions when the greens are about 10 inches (25 cm) tall, before the bulb begins to swell. Carefully pull the onions from moist soil or dig around the bulbs to loosen.

radishes with butter & herbed salt

MAKES 4–6 SERVINGS

There is a reason why this classic French recipe shows up in so many cookbooks—it's lovely! The key to making it special is all in the quality of ingredients. Pluck the radishes from the ground close to serving time or purchase them from the farmers' market the day you plan to serve them.

Trim the radishes, if desired, and leave whole if small, or cut in half if large. Place in a bowl of ice water for 20 minutes.

Pack the butter into a small ramekin or other serving cup. In a small bowl, stir together the salt, tarragon, and crushed pink peppercorns. Put the salt into a small serving cup.

Drain the radishes and pat dry with paper towels, then arrange on a platter along with the butter and salt. Serve the radishes spread with the butter and sprinkled with the salt.

radishes, about 2 dozen

unsalted butter, about ½ cup (4 oz/125 g), at room temperature

sea salt flakes, 2 tbsp

dried tarragon, ½ tsp

pink peppercorns, ½ tsp crushed

herbed cheese & radish crostini

MAKES 12 CROSTINI

This simple hors d'oeuvre tops crostini with herbed cheese and thinly sliced radishes. I like using watermelon radishes here because they are so pretty. I usually use mild, creamy Boursin (the one flavored with garlic and fines herbes), but you can use fresh goat cheese or cream cheese if you prefer.

Preheat the oven to 375°F (190°C). Arrange the baguette slices on a rimmed baking sheet and place in the oven until lightly toasted, 6–8 minutes. Remove from the oven.

Spread the toasts evenly with the cheese, then sprinkle evenly with the chives. Grind a little pepper over each, then top with the radish slices. Arrange the crostini on a platter and serve.

baguette, 12 thin slices

Boursin or fresh goat cheese, 2 oz (60 g)

fresh chives, 2 tsp snipped

freshly ground pepper

radishes, 4 large or 12 small, trimmed and thinly sliced

chicken tostadas with radish slaw

for the chicken

fresh orange juice, ⅔ cup
(5 fl oz/150 ml)

fresh lime juice, 3 tbsp

achiote paste, 3 tbsp

yellow onion, 1 small,
chopped

garlic, 2 cloves, chopped

dried oregano, ½ tsp

boneless, skinless chicken thighs,
2 lb (1 kg)

kosher salt and freshly
ground pepper

for the radish slaw

radishes, 2½ cups (about 18)
trimmed, halved, and thinly sliced

green onions, 2, thinly sliced

fresh cilantro, ⅓ cup (½ oz/15 g)
chopped

fresh lime juice, 1 tbsp

corn oil, for frying

corn tortillas, 12, each 4 inches
(10 cm) in diameter

cotija cheese, 3 oz (90 g),
crumbled

avocados, 2 large, halved,
pitted, peeled, and sliced

Radishes are routinely part of the salsa and condiment spreads available at the best taquerias. Here, I use them as part of a fresh topping for earthy chicken tostadas that is anything but routine. Achiote paste, a popular Yucatecan seasoning made from ground annatto seeds, is available at Mexican stores.

To prepare the chicken, in a heavy Dutch oven, stir together the orange juice, lime juice, and achiote paste until the achiote paste is smooth. Add the onion, garlic, and oregano and mix well. Add the chicken thighs and turn to coat evenly. Sprinkle the chicken with salt.

Cover, place over medium heat, bring to a simmer, then reduce the heat to low and cook, stirring occasionally, until the sauce has thickened and the chicken is opaque throughout when pierced with a knife tip, about 40 minutes. Uncover and continue to simmer until the sauce is very thick and the chicken begins to fall apart and catch on the bottom of the pan, about 10 minutes.

Remove from the heat and let cool slightly, then shred the chicken. Season with salt and pepper.

To make the radish slaw, in a small bowl, combine the radishes, green onions, cilantro, and lime juice and toss to mix. Season with salt.

Pour oil to a depth of 1 inch (2.5 cm) into a deep, heavy frying pan and warm over medium-high heat until almost smoking. One at a time, add the tortillas and cook, turning once with tongs, until crisp and golden, 1–2 minutes. As each tortilla is ready, transfer it to paper towels to drain, then sprinkle lightly with salt.

Arrange 2 tortillas side by side on each individual plate. Top the tortillas with the chicken, dividing it equally, and then spoon the radish slaw evenly over the chicken. Top the tostadas evenly with the cheese and the avocado slices and serve.

At first glance this salad might appear quite plain, but when the mild lettuce, peppery radishes, and snipped chives are topped with tangy old-fashioned buttermilk dressing, you end up with a spring dish that's quite a celebration of flavor and texture. I love pairing this with fried chicken.

To make the dressing, in a jar with a tight-fitting lid, combine the buttermilk, sour cream, mayonnaise, vinegar, chives, garlic, salt, and pepper. Cover tightly and shake vigorously until well blended. You should have about 1⅓ cups (11 fl oz/345 ml). Use right away, or store in an airtight container in the refrigerator for up to 1 week.

Divide the lettuce among 4 individual plates. Scatter the radish slices over the lettuce, dividing the slices evenly. Spoon the dressing to taste over the salads, garnish with chives, and serve.

butter lettuce & radish salad with buttermilk dressing

for the buttermilk dressing

buttermilk, ⅔ cup (5 fl oz/150 ml)

sour cream, ⅓ cup (3 oz/90 g)

mayonnaise, ¼ cup (2 fl oz/60 ml)

cider vinegar, 2 tbsp

fresh chives, 1 tbsp snipped

garlic, 1 clove, pressed

kosher salt, ¾ tsp

freshly ground pepper, ¼ tsp

butter lettuce, 1 head, leaves separated

radishes, 8, trimmed and thinly sliced

snipped fresh chives, for garnish

grilled shrimp & green onions with romesco

for the romesco sauce

piquillo peppers, 1 jar
(about 10½ oz/330 g), drained

almonds, ½ cup (2¾ oz/80 g),
toasted (page 217) and chopped

extra-virgin olive oil,
¼ cup (2 fl oz/60 ml)

garlic, 3 cloves, chopped

smoked paprika, 2 tsp

kosher salt and freshly
ground black pepper

jumbo shrimp, 12, peeled
and deveined

olive oil, 4 tbsp (2 fl oz/60 ml)

garlic cloves, 4, pressed

smoked paprika, 2 tsp

green onions, 16

lemons, 2, halved crosswise

A spring meal of grilled green onions with romesco sauce is an annual tradition in Catalonia. My take on that ritual Spanish meal includes green onions and lemons from my garden and succulent shrimp served with smoky romesco sauce. Sweet piquillo peppers are sold in most specialty-food stores, but roasted red bell peppers can be substituted.

Prepare a medium fire for direct-heat cooking in a charcoal or gas grill.

To make the romesco sauce, in a blender, combine the piquillo peppers, almonds, olive oil, garlic, and paprika and process until smooth. Pour into a bowl and season with salt. Set aside at room temperature.

In a bowl, combine the shrimp, 2 tbsp of the olive oil, the garlic, and the paprika and turn to coat the shrimp evenly. Coat the green onions and lemons lightly with the remaining 2 tbsp olive oil.

Arrange the shrimp on the grill rack directly over the fire and season with salt and black pepper. Cook for about 3 minutes, then add the green onions and lemons, cut side down. Cook, turning all the items as needed, until the shrimp are opaque throughout and the green onions and lemons are lightly charred, about 6 minutes total for the shrimp and 3 minutes total for the green onions and lemons. Transfer the shrimp, green onions, and lemons to a platter and serve with the romesco sauce.

Chives, fennel, parsley, and sorrel are hardy perennials or biennials that are technically summer plants but emerge in early spring, brightening the garden after the gray days of winter. They also bring fresh, green flavor and color to a variety of seasonal dishes, from Mediterranean tabbouleh to simple panfried trout to creamy soups.

how to grow spring herbs

plant and maintain chives

Delicately flavored chives, part of the onion family, are easy to grow from nursery starts and require minimal care. Plant them in well-dug soil in full sun or partial shade about 3 inches (7.5 cm) apart in early spring and water only when dry. Harvest chives throughout the spring and summer and into fall by nipping as much as you need at the base. The plants will die back in most climates, but return each spring, sending up bright green blades in the herb patch. Once your clumps of chives become large and established, you will need to divide them into individual bulbs every 3 or 4 years and replant the bulbs.

plant and maintain fennel

Two types of fennel are grown: Florence fennel, which is grown for its bulb, and common fennel, which is grown for its seeds. To grow common fennel, plant seeds in the garden about 3 inches (7.5 cm) apart—the plant is not picky about the soil or the amount of water or sunshine—after the danger of frost has passed. The seeds will germinate quickly. Thin to about 12 inches (30 cm) apart. As the plants grow and begin to bloom, pinch off the young blossoms and use them in salads. The plant can grow as tall as 4 feet (1.2 m). At the end of the summer, allow the flowers to bloom, then pick and dry them and shake the seeds free. Remember to protect the blossoms from birds, as birds love the seeds too.

Florence fennel can be tricky to grow. Although I have seen fennel starts at my local nursery, it is generally grown from seed. Plant seeds where the fennel is to be grown, about 3 inches (7.5 cm) apart and 1 inch (2.5 cm) deep. Keep the seeds well watered until the first leaves appear, and thin the beginning bulbs to 12 inches (30 cm) apart. The plants prefer cool, moist weather and take about 80 days to yield a mature bulb. I grow a bronze variety, and although it is quite pretty, it never forms a harvestable bulb. I appreciate it primarily for its ornamental value, though bits of the tops make colorful additions to salads.

plant and maintain parsley

Parsley is a biennial, and one of my favorite herbs. It can be grown superfast from nursery starts, or easily and economically from seed. Soak parsley seeds—select the flat-leaf variety for the best flavor and color—in water overnight before sowing. Plant ¼ to ½ inch (6 to 12 mm) deep in full sun, or in partial shade in warmer climates, and keep the soil moist. If you live in an area with a severe winter, start the seeds indoors a few weeks prior to the last predicted frost. Thin or transplant the seedlings to 3 inches (7.5 cm) apart.

plant and maintain sorrel

To cultivate this hardy, rapidly growing perennial, sow seeds in the spring as soon as the ground can be worked (a few weeks before the last frost). Plant them ¼ inch (6 mm) deep and 4 inches (10 cm) apart in well-drained soil in full sun or partial shade. Thin the plants to about 12 inches (30 cm) apart and keep the soil moist at all times. You can cut back the leaves to the ground midsummer to encourage the growth of new, tender leaves. In warm, snow-free climates like mine, this perennial defies its classification and grows year-round.

Bulgur is never boring when mixed with vinaigrette and lots of fresh spring goodies. Try sprinkling it with crumbled feta for a healthy and delicious lunch, or pair it with roasted spring lamb, chicken, or grilled fish for an inspired dinner.

Place the bulgur in a large heatproof bowl. Pour 1 cup (8 fl oz/250 ml) boiling water over the bulgur and let stand for 1 hour. The bulgur will absorb the water.

In a small bowl, whisk together the vinegar, honey, and ½ tsp salt until the honey and salt dissolve. Whisk in the olive oil.

Pour the oil mixture over the bulgur. Add the fennel, green onions, parsley, and sorrel and toss well. Season with pepper, then taste and adjust the seasoning with salt and pepper and serve.

tabbouleh with spring herbs

quick-cooking whole-grain bulgur, 1 cup (6 oz/185 g)

sherry vinegar, 2 tbsp

honey, 1½ tbsp

kosher salt and freshly ground pepper

extra-virgin olive oil, ¼ cup (2 fl oz/60 ml)

fennel bulb, 1, chopped (about 1½ cups/7½ oz/235 g)

green onions, 3, thinly sliced

fresh flat-leaf parsley leaves, ¼ cup (⅓ oz/10 g) chopped

sorrel leaves, ¼ cup (½ oz/15 g) chopped

The first time I tasted sorrel soup was when my boyfriend (now husband) made it for me using the lemony herb from his garden. The recipe was from a James Beard cookbook and was very rich, thickened with cream and eggs. This updated version of the classic French soup, made with less cream and no eggs, is full of the herbaceous flavor of sorrel.

In a large, heavy saucepan over medium heat, melt the butter. Add the green onions and sauté until tender, about 3 minutes. Add the broth and potatoes, bring to a simmer, and simmer, uncovered, until the potatoes are very tender, about 12 minutes.

Stir in the sorrel and parsley, remove from the heat, and let stand until the sorrel softens, about 1 minute. Transfer the mixture to a blender and process until smooth. Add the cream and process briefly to mix.

Return the soup to the saucepan and warm over medium heat, stirring. Season with salt and pepper, ladle into bowls, drizzle with cream, and serve.

potato & sorrel soup

unsalted butter, 1 tbsp

green onions, ½ cup (1½ oz/45 g) sliced

chicken broth, 4 cups (32 fl oz/1 l)

Yukon gold potatoes, 10 oz (315 g), peeled and cut into cubes

sorrel leaves, 1 cup (2 oz/60 g) packed, torn into pieces

fresh flat-leaf parsley leaves, ¼ cup (⅓ oz/10 g) chopped

heavy cream, 2 tbsp, plus more for garnish

kosher salt and freshly ground pepper

fennel seed—crusted chicken with fennel & herb salad

fennel seeds, 1½ tsp

black peppercorns, ¼ tsp

kosher salt and freshly ground black pepper

red pepper flakes, ⅛ tsp

boneless, skinless chicken breast halves, 2

extra-virgin olive oil, 4 tsp

fennel bulb, ½ small, shaved (about ½ cup/2 oz/60 g)

fresh chives, 2 tbsp, snipped

fresh flat-leaf parsley leaves, 2 tbsp

fennel tops, 1 tbsp, chopped

fresh lemon juice, 1 tbsp

dry rosé, ¼ cup (2 fl oz/60 ml)

chicken broth, ¼ cup (2 fl oz/60 ml)

MAKES 2 SERVINGS

Use a V-slicer or mandoline to thinly slice or shave the fennel for this salad. I like to serve a dry rosé with this dish, which is why I use rosé in the pan sauce. If you prefer, you can use a dry white wine.

In a mortar, using a pestle, grind together the fennel seeds, peppercorns, ¼ tsp salt, and red pepper flakes until coarsely ground. Place 1 chicken breast between 2 sheets of plastic wrap and pound lightly with a meat mallet until evenly flattened to ½ inch (12 mm) thick. Repeat with the second chicken breast.

In a large, well-seasoned (or nonstick) frying pan over medium-high heat, warm 2 tsp of the olive oil. Sprinkle both sides of the chicken breasts evenly with the fennel seed mixture and add to the skillet. Cook, turning once, until golden brown on both sides and just cooked through, 3–4 minutes on each side.

Meanwhile, stir together the shaved fennel, chives, parsley, fennel tops, lemon juice, and the remaining 2 tsp olive oil in a medium bowl and season to taste with salt and black pepper.

Transfer the chicken breasts to warmed plates. Add the rosé and broth to the frying pan and simmer until reduced by about half, about 1 minute. Pour the pan juices over the chicken and top each with some of the fennel-herb salad, dividing evenly. Serve.

panfried trout with brown butter, hazelnuts & parsley

I bring a large iron skillet and all the ingredients, save for the trout, when I go camping in the mountains in the hope I'll catch dinner. If the fishing doesn't pan out, I stop at the market for trout on the way home. Browned butter enhances all the flavors in this simple dish, and hazelnuts and parsley bring out the sweetness of the trout. When browning butter, cook it until it is a nut brown—but no longer.

In a large, heavy frying pan over medium heat, melt the butter. Cook the butter, swirling the pan occasionally, until it is nut brown, about 5 minutes. Watch carefully so that it does not burn. Pour off the butter into a small bowl, leaving a thin layer in the pan. Add the hazelnuts to the pan and stir over medium heat until golden brown, about 3 minutes. Transfer the nuts to another small bowl.

Warm the same pan (do not rinse it) over medium-high heat. Add 2 tsp of the browned butter to the pan. When the butter is hot, add the trout. Cook, turning once, until browned on both sides and the flesh just flakes when prodded with a knife tip near the backbone, about 4 minutes on each side. Transfer the trout to a warmed platter and cover with aluminum foil to keep warm.

Return the pan to medium heat, add the shallots, and sauté until tender, about 2 minutes. Add the wine and lemon juice and simmer until reduced by half, about 1 minute. Whisk in the browned butter remaining in the bowl and the lemon zest.

Remove the sauce from the heat and stir in the parsley. Pour the sauce over the trout, sprinkle with the hazelnuts, and serve.

unsalted butter, ¼ cup (2 oz/60 g)

hazelnuts, 3 tbsp chopped

rainbow trout, 2, about 7 oz (220 g) each, dressed

shallots, ¼ cup (1½ oz/45 g) minced

white wine, ¼ cup (2 fl oz/60 ml)

fresh lemon juice, 3 tbsp

lemon zest, ½ tsp grated

fresh flat-leaf parsley leaves, ¼ cup (⅓ oz/10 g) chopped

In some regions, strawberries are the first fruit after winter, in others they are everbearing perennials, and in colder climes they are the harbinger of summer. But mostly, strawberries symbolize spring.

how to grow strawberries

plant and maintain strawberries

If you want more than the occasional warm-off-the-vine perfect berry, you will need to allow plenty of space for your strawberry crop. I have a cute terra-cotta strawberry pot with about 6 plants sprouting from its pockets, and it yields only about a dozen berries a season. Select a patch with loamy soil and at least 90 days of full sun. Strawberry varieties are available for most gardening zones, but the plants do best where the nights are cool and the air is moist. Plant crowns on small mounds about 6 inches (15 cm) high and 2 feet (60 cm) apart. Cover the roots with soil and leave the crowns exposed to sunlight (to avoid rot). Water frequently and weed vigilantly, as uninvited invaders can overtake plants quickly. Also, bugs like sweet berries just as much as we do, so hunt down offenders, especially pill bugs, and exterminate them organically. I feed them to my chickens. Feed plants twice a year, first when new growth appears in early spring or winter, and then again after fruiting is finished. Use a complete, balanced fertilizer such as 10-10-10. If well cared for, the plants will produce for a few years.

harvest strawberries

During the plant's first year, pinch off some of the first blossoms in order to encourage vigorous plant growth. Later in the season, harvest berries as soon as they become ripe, before the birds or bugs get them. You can follow the lead of commercial growers and treat strawberries like annuals—planting new plants in the spring and pulling them out and composting them after harvest—but you will need to find a new planting area as you shouldn't replant in the same area for at least two years as the soil will not be suitable. This method results in bushy plants and high yield.

lemon-kissed strawberry jam

strawberries, 1 lb (500 g), stemmed and cored

sugar, ½ cup (4 oz/125 g)

lemon zest, ½ tsp grated

fresh lemon juice, 1 tsp

MAKES ABOUT 1 HALF-PINT (8—FL OZ/250-ML) JAR

This is a small-batch recipe: it makes just one perfect jar. Use surplus berries from the garden (or from the farmers' market) to make a jar when you can, then enjoy it with toast and biscuits in late spring, with butter cookies in summer, and with peanut butter for back-to-school lunches in fall.

Put the berries in a heavy saucepan. Using a potato masher, roughly mash them, leaving some berries whole. Place over medium heat and cook, stirring occasionally, until reduced to about 1 cup (10 oz/315 g), about 12 minutes.

Meanwhile, in a small bowl, rub the sugar and lemon zest together between your fingertips to release the essential oils in the zest.

When the strawberries are ready, add the lemon sugar and continue cooking, stirring frequently, until the mixture thickens and is reduced again to 1 cup (10 oz/315 g), about 6 minutes. Stir in the lemon juice. Transfer the jam to a clean jar, cap tightly, and refrigerate. It will keep for up to 2 weeks.

strawberries with honey & lavender

strawberries, 2 lb (1 kg)

sugar, 1 rounded tbsp

dried lavender blossoms, ¼ tsp

honey, 2 tbsp

crème fraîche, for serving

MAKES 6 SERVINGS

You might not think that juicy, sweet strawberries need any embellishment, but a hint of honey and lavender adds a touch of perfume, and the strawberries actually enhance the flavors of the lavender and honey. If you have lavender blooming in your garden, use fresh blossoms instead.

Stem and core the strawberries, then halve small ones or quarter large ones lengthwise. Place in a large bowl.

In a mortar, using a pestle, grind together the sugar and lavender blossoms until the lavender is finely ground. Sprinkle the lavender sugar over the strawberries, then drizzle the honey over the berries. Stir to coat the berries evenly. Serve in small bowls with a dollop of crème fraîche.

strawberry hazelnut shortcakes

These shortcakes are delicate, so you need to use a serrated knife and a gentle sawing motion to split them. Or you can set a whole biscuit alongside a big scoop of the berries topped with cream. I like the sweet, earthy flavor of hazelnuts here, but toasted walnuts or pecans would be great too.

Preheat the oven to 400°F (200°C). Line a large, heavy baking sheet with a silicone baking mat or parchment paper.

In a food processor, combine the flour, brown sugar, baking powder, and salt and pulse a few times to mix. Scatter the butter over the flour mixture and pulse until the mixture resembles coarse meal. Add the hazelnuts and pulse until the hazelnuts are finely chopped. Pour the cream evenly over the mixture and pulse until moist clumps form.

Remove the dough from the processor, gather into a ball, and place the ball on a lightly floured work surface. Pat the dough into a 4-by-6-inch (10-by-15-cm) rectangle. Using a sharp knife, cut the rectangle into 2-inch (5-cm) squares, making 6 biscuits total (with no scraps).

Transfer the biscuits to the prepared baking sheet. Brush the tops with cream and sprinkle with the turbinado sugar. Bake the biscuits until they are golden brown and cooked through, about 14 minutes. Let cool completely on the pan on a wire rack.

Split each biscuit and place on individual plates. Spoon the berries and cream onto the bottom halves, cap with the biscuit tops, and serve.

unbleached all-purpose flour, 1½ cups (7½ oz/235 g)

golden brown sugar, ⅓ cup (2½ oz/75 g) firmly packed

baking powder, 2 tsp

kosher salt, ½ tsp

unsalted butter, 6 tbsp (3 oz/90 g) cold, cut into 6 pieces

hazelnuts, ⅔ cup (3 oz/90 g), toasted (page 217)

heavy cream, ½ cup (4 fl oz/ 125 ml) cold, plus more for brushing

turbinado sugar, for sprinkling

strawberries with honey and lavender (page 68)

vanilla whipped cream (page 217)

SUMMER

tomatoes crimson caramelo, georgia streak, paul robeson, yellow brandywine, early girl, better boy, sungold cherry, chocolate cherry, sweet 100s, green zebra • **cucumbers** spacemaster, persian, lemon **summer squashes** romanesco zucchini, golden zucchini, ronde de nice, black beauty zucchini, pattypan • **snap & shell beans** ramdor, emerite, golden roc d'or, purple queen, green slenderette, scarlet emperor runner bean, missouri wonder, black eyed peas, cow peas **basil** napolitano, genovese, lemon, red osmin, siam queen • **lavender** english, hidcote, munstead • **mint** kentucky colonel spearmint, golden apple mint, chocolate mint • **oregano** greek, mexican, wild **tarragon** french • **raspberries** bababerry, caroline, chilcotin, fallred, kiska, summit • **blackberries** jewel, royalty • **blueberries** chippewa, bluecrop, polaris • **stone fruits** elberta peach, midpride peach, nectar peach, arctic rose nectarine, le grand nectarine, autumn royal apricot, blenheim apricot, late santa rosa plum, burbank plum, seneca plum, emerald beauty plum

SUMMER

Summer's official start date is June 22, and by then, your summer garden will already be established. That's because many summer vegetables and fruits, such as tomatoes, zucchini, cucumbers, green beans, and berries, went into the ground months earlier, and others, such as stone fruits, were planted at least a year ahead. Summer crops are some of the easiest to grow, as they produce the most for the amount of labor and water you invest in them during the season.

Cooks have no trouble coming up with ways to use the summer's bountiful harvests. Cucumbers are turned into pickles or puréed into a soup, and herbs such as basil, mint, and lavender are whipped into a pesto, steeped to make tea, or dried to use the rest of the year. Tomatoes, a favorite of nearly every gardener and cook, are used to top pizzas and make salads and sauces. Berries and stone fruits are transformed into tarts and crisps, jams and chutneys, and luscious ice creams.

taking care of your garden

Just as many of us spend time in the summer looking for respite from the heat, we need to make sure our garden grows and thrives, rather than wilts and dies during the season's long, hot days. Regular watering, mulching, removing spent leaves, and harvesting are things we can do to keep the garden flourishing. Fortunately, the warm, long days make performing these tasks a pleasure, especially if a juicy tomato or peach is the reward.

WATERING During the heat of summer, it's important to water deeply and thoroughly. When you water, be careful to avoid sprinkling the foliage in the heat of the day, which can cause burning, and at the end of the day, which can encourage mildew. To make sure you are watering effectively, check your soil moisture from time to time by digging about 4 inches (10 cm) deep into your garden bed to make sure the ground is damp. Try to maintain a regular watering schedule, keeping in mind that morning hours are the most pleasant for you and your plants.

MULCHING Mulch is a protective cover placed over the soil to retain moisture, add nutrients, and prevent erosion and weed germination. Mulch comes in many forms, with hay, pine needles, newspaper, wool, shells, and wood chips among them. For vegetable gardens, I prefer organic, partially composted mulch, often labeled "aged compost mulch." Select a mulch with a fine consistency to avoid incorporating large sticks and chunks of wood into your soil.

HARVESTING Harvest your fruits and vegetables as they ripen. This may seem obvious, but during the summer's super-growing season, vegetables such as zucchini and tomatoes have a way of getting away from you. A zucchini can go from perfect to gigantic seemingly overnight, and when tomatoes are at their peak, they ripen quickly and are often shrouded by foliage, forcing you to play a little hide-and-seek.

Climbers like cucumbers and beans actually produce more fruit the more you pick because the plant isn't putting all its energy into making seeds. These plants also have a short season, which makes them perfect for planting in succession. By sowing seeds or planting nursery starts every couple of weeks through July, you'll be able to harvest crunchy cucumbers and snappy beans all summer long.

PLANTING Although summer is primarily a time of reaping rewards and keeping plants alive and thriving, as the days shorten, some new planting can be done. In colder zones, the end of summer means sowing carrot and beet seeds for fall and winter harvest, and in warm zones, the end of the summer is a good time to plant sweet potatoes.

Tomatoes are my favorite vegetable to grow. A freshly picked, vine-ripened home-grown tomato has no equal. Even fancy farmers' market heirlooms don't hold a candle to my backyard beauties, which I use for everything from pizza toppings and long-simmered ragùs to salads, soups, and even jam. At the beginning of the season, I like them best simply sliced and sprinkled with salt.

how to grow tomatoes

select and plant tomatoes

Purchase plants in 4-inch (10-cm) pots from a nursery. I have tried to grow tomatoes from seed, but without a greenhouse, the seedlings never mature quickly enough at the optimum time to flourish. I plant both hybrid and heirloom, or open-pollinated, tomatoes. Heirloom tomatoes are cultivated from seeds that have been saved from previous seasons' plants and reproduce true to type. They have excellent flavor and texture and vary significantly in size, color, shape, and taste. Hybrid tomatoes, which are not without their virtues, are crossbred for specific attributes, such as disease resistance, firmness, and transportability. Unlike heirlooms, hybrids do not reproduce true to the parent plant. They are my "backup plan." If bad weather, pests, or disease affect the more susceptible heirlooms, I still have my tasty Lemon Boys and Early Girls.

Plant tomato starts in May or when the temperature in your area is consistently above 50°F (10°C) and all threat of frost has past. Tomatoes like full sun and well-draining, rich, loose soil. Space the plants 2 to 3 feet (60 to 90 cm) apart, and cover the stems with 3 to 4 inches (7.5 to 10 cm) of soil. Deep planting ensures that the tomatoes will have a strong root structure that will keep the plant stable and strong.

maintain tomatoes

Tomatoes grow best when watered deeply and consistently. Don't allow the soil to become dry between waterings, and always dig into the soil to make sure the dirt is evenly and deeply saturated. Avoid getting the foliage wet, as damp leaves can mildew and cause disease.

Stake or cage the tomato plants. I prefer cages, which encourage the plants to grow in and around the wires that will help support future branches and fruits. The fruits are ripe when they yield to gentle pressure. Be sure to monitor green varieties closely. Color is no indicator of ripeness, and it's easy to be taken by surprise by overripe or fallen fruit.

harvest tomatoes

Use kitchen shears or small, sharp clippers to cut the ripe fruit at the base of the stem. Don't pull tomatoes off the plant. You might damage the fruit or break the stem, which could be supporting other not-yet-ripe tomatoes. Store tomatoes in a basket in a cool area of the kitchen. Unblemished fruit will keep for 2 or 3 days.

tomato jam with honey & marjoram

red tomatoes, 3 lb (1.5 kg)

shallot, ⅓ cup (1½ oz/45 g) minced

red pepper flakes, ⅛ tsp

golden brown sugar, ¼ cup (2 oz/60 g) firmly packed

granulated sugar, ¼ cup (2 oz/60 g)

honey, 2 tbsp

sherry vinegar, 1 tbsp

fresh marjoram, 2 tbsp chopped

Each spring I plant both heirloom and hybrid tomatoes. The hybrids are an "insurance policy" in case a pest or disease knocks out the more sensitive heirlooms. This sweet-savory jam makes great use of my Better Boy and Early Girl hybrids. Try serving the jam atop baguette slices spread with Bûcheron or another fresh goat cheese.

Bring a large saucepan three-fourths full of water to a boil. Meanwhile, using a small, sharp knife, cut out the stem from each tomato, then cut a small, shallow X on the blossom end. Working in small batches, immerse the tomatoes in the boiling water until the skins blister, about 30 seconds. As they are ready, using a slotted spoon, transfer the tomatoes to a colander.

Working over a bowl, peel the tomatoes, discarding the skins. Using your fingers, break the tomatoes open and gently squeeze and scrape the seeds and juices into the bowl. Transfer the flesh to a small, heavy saucepan. Strain the juices through a fine-mesh sieve into the pan, discarding the seeds.

Add the shallot and red pepper flakes to the tomatoes, place the pan over medium heat, bring to a simmer, and simmer until the mixture is reduced to 2 cups (12 oz/375 g), about 12 minutes. Add both sugars, the honey, and the vinegar and continue to simmer, stirring often, until the mixture is thickened to a jam consistency, about 7 minutes.

Remove from the heat and stir in the marjoram. Transfer the jam to clean jars, let cool, cap tightly, and refrigerate. It will keep for up to 2 weeks.

tomato gazpacho with roasted pepper, cucumber & avocado

You can use any combination of tomatoes in this luscious Spanish soup. I find it an excellent way to use up all of my less-than-perfect tomatoes—ones with splits, soft spots, or cracks. I just cut out the blemishes and proceed with the recipe. Enjoy the soup as a starter or light lunch.

Using tongs, hold 1 bell pepper over the flame of a gas burner, turning it as needed, until charred and blistered on all sides. Repeat with the second pepper. Alternatively, preheat the broiler, place the peppers on a baking sheet, and broil, turning as needed, until blackened on all sides. Place the bell peppers in a small bowl, cover the bowl with plastic wrap, and leave until cool. Peel off the blackened skin and remove the stem and seeds. Set aside.

Bring a large saucepan three-fourths full of water to a boil. Using a small, sharp knife, cut out the stem from each tomato, then cut a small, shallow X on the blossom end. Working in small batches, immerse the tomatoes in the boiling water until the skins blister, about 30 seconds. As they are ready, using a slotted spoon, transfer the tomatoes to a large colander.

Working over a bowl, peel the tomatoes, discarding the skins. Using your fingers, break the tomatoes open and gently squeeze and scrape the seeds and juices into the bowl. Transfer the flesh to another bowl. Using a fine-mesh sieve, strain the juices into the bowl with the tomato flesh. Discard the seeds.

Working in batches, in a blender, combine the tomato flesh and juice, 1 roasted bell pepper, and the cucumbers, garlic, olive oil, vinegar, and salt. Process until smooth, then transfer to a bowl. Seed, stem, and finely dice the remaining bell pepper, and stir into the tomato mixture. Cover and refrigerate until well chilled, about 2 hours.

Taste and adjust the seasoning with salt, then divide among chilled bowls. Garnish with the avocado, drizzle with a little olive oil, and serve.

red bell peppers, 2

tomatoes, preferably heirloom, 5 lb (2.5 kg)

cucumbers, 2 small or one 8-inch (20-cm) piece of larger cucumber, peeled, seeded, and coarsely chopped

garlic, 2 cloves, coarsely chopped

extra-virgin olive oil, ¼ cup (2 fl oz/60 ml), plus more for finishing

sherry vinegar, 2 tsp

kosher salt, 1 tsp

avocado, 1 large, pitted, peeled, and chopped

rustic tomato, arugula & bread salad

coarse country bread, ½ lb (250 g), thickly sliced

garlic, 1 large clove

heirloom tomatoes, 2 lb (1 kg)

Persian cucumbers, 2 small

red onion, ½, sliced paper-thin

capers, 2 tbsp

extra-virgin olive oil, 6 tbsp (3 fl oz/90 ml)

red wine vinegar, 2 tbsp

kosher salt, ½ tsp

arugula, 1½ cups (1½ oz/45 g), torn

fresh basil leaves, 3 tbsp, torn

fresh oregano leaves, 2 tbsp

freshly ground pepper

Parmesan cheese, 2 oz (60 g), shaved

Preheat the oven to 375°F (190°C). Arrange the bread slices on a rimmed baking sheet. Toast in the oven, turning once, until golden brown, about 5 minutes. Remove from the oven and let cool slightly, then rub the bread slices on both sides with the garlic clove.

Slice the tomatoes into thin wedges. Halve the cucumbers lengthwise, then thinly slice them crosswise.

In a large serving bowl, combine the tomatoes, cucumbers, onion, capers, olive oil, vinegar, and salt. Tear the bread into 1-inch (2.5-cm) pieces and add to the bowl. Stir to combine and let stand until the bread is soft and soaked with tomato juices, about 10 minutes.

Add the arugula, basil, and oregano to the salad and toss to combine. Season with pepper, garnish with the cheese shavings, and serve.

oven-roasted tomatoes with herbs

extra-virgin olive oil, 2 tbsp, plus more for baking sheet

small round or plum tomatoes, 2 lb (1 kg), halved through the stem end

garlic, 2 cloves, pressed

fresh oregano leaves, 1 tbsp minced

fresh thyme leaves, 2 tsp minced

kosher salt, ¼ tsp

Roasting intensifies the flavor of tomatoes, and these are fantastic with roast meats or sautéed fish or in sandwiches or salads. Chilled, drizzled with olive oil and balsamic vinegar, and paired with Brie, they make an elegant starter. They can also be puréed and used as a tasty sauce on pizza or pasta.

Preheat the oven to 375°F (190°C). Brush a large, heavy rimmed baking sheet with olive oil. In a bowl, toss together the tomatoes, oil, garlic, oregano, and thyme. Arrange the tomatoes, cut sides up, on the prepared baking sheet. Sprinkle the tomatoes with the salt. Roast the tomatoes until they are soft and beginning to brown, about 50 minutes. Let the tomatoes cool to room temperature on the baking sheet. Serve at room temperature or chilled.

grilled pizza with cherry tomatoes & gorgonzola

cherry tomatoes, 1½ cups (9 oz/280 g), stemmed and halved

extra-virgin olive oil, 2 tbsp, plus more for brushing

garlic, 2 cloves, pressed

kosher salt

unbleached all-purpose flour, for dusting

pizza dough (page 215), about ¾ lb (340 g)

whole-milk mozzarella cheese, 1¼ cups (5 oz/155 g) shredded

Gorgonzola cheese, ¼ lb (125 g), crumbled

green onions, 2, thinly sliced

fresh basil leaves, 2 tbsp chopped

fresh marjoram or oregano leaves, 1 tbsp chopped

If you prefer, you can thinly slice 2 large tomatoes for this pizza. Just make sure that you remove the excess seeds and moisture from the slices so your pizza doesn't become soggy. If you're pressed for time, you can make the pizza with purchased dough, available at many specialty-food markets.

In a bowl, combine the tomatoes, 1 tbsp of the olive oil, and 1 garlic clove. Sprinkle with salt and stir to blend. In a small bowl, mix the remaining garlic clove with the remaining 1 tbsp olive oil.

Prepare a medium fire for direct-heat cooking in a charcoal or gas grill.

Meanwhile, on a lightly floured work surface, roll out the dough into a rectangle about 11 by 13 inches (28 by 33 cm). Brush the top surface of the dough with olive oil.

Place the dough on the grill, oiled side down, and immediately brush the top of the crust with the garlic oil. Grill until well browned on the bottom, about 5 minutes. Using a wide spatula, carefully turn the pizza crust over, and immediately sprinkle with the mozzarella and Gorgonzola cheeses. Distribute the tomato mixture evenly over the cheeses, and sprinkle evenly with the green onions, basil, and marjoram. Grill until the pizza is just browned on the bottom and the cheeses melt, about 7 minutes.

Using the spatula or a rimless baking sheet, transfer the pizza to a cutting board. Cut the pizza into squares and serve.

heirloom tomato & watermelon salad with feta & mint

mini seedless watermelon, about 4 lb (2 kg)

heirloom tomatoes, 1¾ lb (875 g), sliced

Persian cucumbers, 2, sliced

extra-virgin olive oil, 2 tbsp

white balsamic vinegar, 2 tbsp

feta cheese, 3 oz (90 g), crumbled

fresh mint leaves, ½ cup (½ oz/15 g)

MAKES 6 SERVINGS

I like to use yellow tomatoes for this dish because they are so visually striking against the dark pink of the watermelon. The combination of flavors and textures in this cooling salad is superb. Enjoy it as a starter or as a side dish to grilled shrimp.

Remove the rind from the watermelon and cut into 3-inch (7.5-cm) wedges, then thinly slice the wedges.

In a large shallow serving bowl, gently toss together the watermelon, tomato, and cucumber slices. Drizzle the olive oil and vinegar over the mixture, sprinkle with feta and mint, and serve.

zucchini, tomato & pepper ragout with polenta

extra-virgin olive oil, 2 tbsp

yellow onion, 1 small, chopped

red, yellow, or orange bell pepper, 1, seeded and sliced

green chile such as Anaheim, Hatch, or poblano, 1 large, seeded and sliced

red or plum tomatoes, 1½ lb (750 g), chopped

mixed fresh herbs such as thyme, basil, oregano, or marjoram, ¼ cup (⅓ oz/10 g) chopped, plus 2 tbsp

garlic, 4 cloves, chopped

zucchini or crookneck squash, 2, trimmed and cut into slices ¼ inch (6 mm) thick

cherry tomatoes, 1 cup (6 oz/185 g), stemmed

creamy polenta (page 216)

grated Parmesan cheese, for serving

MAKES 4 SERVINGS

This is a great way to put the produce from a small summer garden to use in a boldly flavored vegetarian main course. I like to use a mixture of herbs—plucking a few basil leaves and oregano and thyme sprigs from my plants. The sauce is also good spooned over pasta tossed with olive oil.

In a large, heavy frying pan over medium heat, warm the olive oil. Add the onion, bell pepper, and chile and sauté until tender, about 12 minutes. Add the red tomatoes and sauté until tender and saucy, 7–8 minutes. Stir in ¼ cup of the herbs and the garlic and cook, stirring, for 1 minute. Add the zucchini and cherry tomatoes, cover, and cook until the zucchini is tender and the cherry tomatoes have burst, about 5 minutes.

Uncover and stir briefly. Divide the polenta among warmed shallow bowls. Spoon the ragout over the polenta, dividing it evenly, and sprinkle with the remaining herbs and the cheese. Serve.

Cucumbers require more attention than squashes in the garden, but with a little TLC, you'll enjoy them all summer long in salads, soups, and as snacks, either straight off the vine or as tart, crunchy pickles. Summer squashes are equally versatile: young and tender, they can be eaten raw; more mature specimens can be sautéed, grilled, baked, roasted, broiled, or even grated and folded into cake or muffin batter.

how to grow summer vines

plant and maintain cucumbers

Most cucumbers are climbers, though some specialty growers sell "bush" varieties. Three general types are available: slicing, pickling, and gherkin. Small pickling cukes, slender, dark-skinned Japanese and Persian cucumbers, and round, yellow, juicy lemon cucumbers are my favorite varieties to grow.

Plant seeds or nursery starts in rich, well-cultivated soil in raised beds, on small mounds, or in large pots in late spring, or as soon as the ground has warmed after winter. Sow seeds ½ to 1 inch (12 mm to 2.5 cm) deep and 6 to 12 inches (15 to 30 cm) apart, depending on your plot or container size. Space nursery starts the same distance. Be sure to plant more than one cucumber vine to ensure pollination. The fruits can reach maturity in as quickly as 40 days, so if you live where spring arrives early, you can put in two crops throughout the season.

Cucumbers like moist, warm soil. In cooler climes, surround the seedlings with black plastic sheeting to warm the soil and speed growth. In hotter areas, mulch to keep the soil moist. As cucumbers appear, train the plants onto trellises or tomato cages. I plant cucumbers next to tomatoes and allow the vines to intertwine with the tomato plants. Once the plants begin to vine, apply nitrogen-rich fertilizer.

harvest cucumbers

Pick cucumbers as they ripen. Failure to harvest them will cause the plant to stop producing, wither, and die—the more cucumbers you pick, the more will grow.

plant and maintain summer squashes

Zucchini, straightneck, and crookneck are among the best squashes to grow. Two types of plants are available, bush and vine, so if your garden is small, opt for a bush variety. Plant seeds or nursery starts on small mounds or in raised beds. If planting seeds, cover them with about 1 inch (2.5 cm) of soil, and plant two or three times the number of plants you want. Once they germinate, thin the weaker seedlings. Water regularly and deeply, being careful not to get the leaves wet, which can encourage disease. As the plants begin to blossom and produce fruits, begin feeding them every 2 to 3 weeks with a balanced, general-purpose fertilizer.

harvest summer squashes

Be sure to pick the squashes before they develop thick, tough skins, checking under the leaves for torpedo-size sneakers.

cucumber refrigerator pickles with dill & lemon

coriander seeds, 2 tbsp

fresh dill sprigs, 4 large

lemon, 1 small, sliced

pickling or other small cucumbers, 3, about ¾ lb (375 g) total weight, cut into slices ¼ inch (6 mm) thick

cider vinegar, ¾ cup (6 fl oz/180 ml)

honey, 2 tbsp

kosher salt, 2 tsp

Refrigerator pickles are fun and easy to make. I make them throughout the summer, varying the recipe slightly each time. The following brine is a winner, but feel free to adapt the recipe to your taste: a little more honey if you like sweet pickles, or some garlic, dried red chiles, and peppercorns if you want some heat. The pickles are ready to eat—mild and crunchy—after 1 day and will get more "pickled" as they sit.

In a heavy frying pan over medium-high heat, toast the coriander seeds, shaking the pan often, until they are lightly browned and fragrant, about 30 seconds. Transfer the seeds to a small bowl and let cool.

Sprinkle 1½ tsp of the coriander seeds in the bottom of a 1-qt (1-l) jar. Top with a dill sprig and a couple of lemon slices. Top with one-third of the cucumber slices. Repeat the layering twice. Push the remaining dill, lemon slices, and coriander seeds into the jar.

To make the brine, in a measuring pitcher, stir together 1 cup (8 fl oz/ 250 ml) water with the vinegar, honey, and salt until the honey and salt dissolve. Pour the brine into the jar. If it does not cover the ingredients completely, top with additional water as needed.

Cap the jar tightly and refrigerate overnight before serving. Discard the brine and enjoy the pickles within a day or two. After about 5 days, the pickles are usually too vinegary.

shaved zucchini salad with almonds & asiago

extra-virgin olive oil,
¼ cup (2 fl oz/60 ml)

fresh lemon juice, 2 tbsp

garlic, 1 clove, pressed

kosher salt and freshly
ground pepper

zucchini, ¾ lb (375 g), trimmed

fresh flat-leaf parsley leaves,
¼ cup (⅓ oz/10 g) chopped

baby arugula leaves,
1 cup (1 oz/30 g)

Asiago cheese, 1 oz (30 g),
shaved

almonds, 2 tbsp, toasted
(page 217) and chopped

MAKES 4 SERVINGS

Midway through summer, after I've enjoyed plenty of zucchini—sautéed, grilled, puréed in soup, and shredded in pancakes—I'm ready for a change but still flush with zukes. Shaving raw zucchini for this pretty salad is inspired relief! I like to use a mixture of green and golden zucchini; be sure to choose long, narrow squashes for the best ribbons. Serve it as an elegant starter or a light side dish to grilled fish.

In a large, shallow serving bowl, whisk together the olive oil, lemon juice, garlic, and ¼ tsp salt until the salt dissolves.

To make the zucchini ribbons, using a vegetable peeler, shave long strips of squash from the stem to the blossom end. Continue making ribbons until half of the zucchini is shaved, then turn the zucchini over and continue shaving ribbons from the opposite side. Transfer the ribbons to the bowl with the dressing.

Add the parsley to the zucchini, season with salt and pepper, and toss gently. Gently toss the arugula into the zucchini mixture, garnish with the cheese and almonds, and serve.

zucchini griddle cakes with feta & mint

large eggs, 4

garlic, 2 cloves, pressed

kosher salt, ½ tsp

freshly ground pepper, ½ tsp

unbleached all-purpose flour,
½ cup (2½ oz/75 g)

zucchini or crookneck squash,
1½ lb (750 g), trimmed and
coarsely grated

green onions, 2 cups (6 oz/185 g)
chopped

fresh basil leaves, ⅓ cup
(½ oz/15 g) chopped

fresh mint leaves, ⅓ cup
(½ oz/15 g) chopped

feta cheese, 1 cup (5 oz/155 g)
crumbled

extra-virgin olive oil, 1–2 tbsp

MAKES 4–8 SERVINGS

Even if you tend your summer vegetable plot diligently, you often discover a zucchini that seems to have gotten huge overnight. When that happens to me, I make these delicious griddle cakes. I serve them with yogurt as a vegetarian main course, as an appetizer, or as part of a meze platter. Don't mix the batter until just before you are ready to cook it.

In a large bowl, whisk together the eggs, garlic, salt, and pepper until well blended. Whisk in the flour. Stir in the zucchini, green onions, basil, and mint. Gently mix in the feta cheese.

On a griddle or a well-seasoned cast-iron frying pan over medium-high heat, warm enough olive oil to create a thin layer. For each cake, drop a scant ¼ cup (2 fl oz/60 ml) of the batter onto the hot surface, spacing the cakes evenly. Cook until golden brown on the bottom, about 3 minutes. Carefully turn the cakes and continue cooking until golden brown on the second side, about 3 minutes longer.

Transfer the cakes to a platter and cover to keep warm. Repeat with the remaining batter, adding more olive oil to the pan as needed to prevent sticking. Serve.

You can find many different takes on cucumber soup, but this dairy-free version, made with almond milk, is particularly light and refreshing and reminds me of the chilled Spanish almond and garlic soup, *ajo blanco*.

Peel the cucumbers and cut in half lengthwise. Run a spoon down the center of the cut side of each half to remove the seeds. Cut the cucumbers into chunks. You should have about 3½ cups (17½ oz/545 g).

In a blender, combine the cucumbers, green onion, chopped mint, chile, and garlic and process until smooth. Add the almond milk and salt and process until well blended. Transfer to a bowl, cover, and refrigerate until well chilled, about 2 hours. (The soup can be refrigerated for up to 10 hours before serving.)

Whisk the soup briefly to blend, then taste and adjust the seasoning. Divide the soup among chilled bowls, garnish with the mint, and serve.

chilled cucumber soup with mint

cucumbers, 2 large or 4 small

green onion, ¼ cup (¾ oz/20 g) sliced

fresh mint leaves, 2 tbsp chopped, plus small leaves for garnish

jalapeño chile, 2 tsp seeded and chopped

garlic, 1 clove

unsweetened almond milk, 2 cups (16 fl oz/500 ml) cold

kosher salt, ½ tsp

MAKES 4–6 SERVINGS

This is my go-to when I crave something salty and crunchy. It's so satisfying and so much better for me than a bag of chips! Japanese and Persian cucumbers are long and narrow with a tender skin and a delicate sweetness that's enhanced by the salty miso dressing.

In a bowl, whisk together the miso, vinegar, sesame oil, and brown sugar until well blended. Add the cucumbers and green onion, stir gently to coat with the dressing, and serve.

cucumber salad with miso dressing

white miso, 2 tbsp

rice vinegar, 2 tbsp

Asian sesame oil, 2 tsp

golden brown sugar, ½ tsp firmly packed

small Japanese or Persian cucumbers, 2 lb (1 kg), thinly sliced

green onions, 2, thinly sliced

grilled squash & sausages with sauce verte

Bright-tasting *sauce verte* (green sauce) perks up the sausages and squash in this summery grilled meal. I like to serve sliced tomatoes on a bed of greens and rustic bread with this dish and enjoy the sauce on everything. The sauce is also great with grilled chicken and fish.

To make the sauce, in a food processor, combine the basil, green onion, parsley, capers, lemon juice, oregano, mustard, and garlic and process until finely chopped. With the processor running, slowly pour in the olive oil and process until the mixture forms a chunky purée. (The sauce can be covered and refrigerated for up to 3 days.)

Prepare a medium fire for direct-heat cooking in a charcoal or gas grill.

Brush the squash halves with olive oil and season on all sides with salt and pepper. Arrange the squash halves and sausages on the grill directly over the fire and grill, turning as needed, until the squash halves are just tender when pierced with a sharp knife, about 4 minutes. Transfer the squash halves to a platter, and toss with about ⅓ cup (3 fl oz/80 ml) of the sauce. Continue grilling the sausages, turning as needed, until cooked through, about 4 minutes longer.

Transfer the sausages to the platter with the squash, sprinkle with the parsley, and serve. Pass the remaining sauce at the table.

for the sauce verte

fresh basil leaves, ⅓ cup (1 oz/30 g) packed

green onion, 1, coarsely chopped

fresh flat-leaf parsley leaves, 2 tbsp packed

capers, 2 tbsp

fresh lemon juice, 1 tbsp

fresh oregano leaves, 1 tbsp

Dijon mustard, 2 tsp

garlic, 1 clove, coarsely chopped

extra-virgin olive oil, 3 tbsp

summer squash such as pattypan, zucchini, or crookneck, 2 lb (1 kg), trimmed and halved lengthwise

extra-virgin olive oil, for brushing

kosher salt and freshly ground pepper

French garlic or hot Italian sausages, 6, about 1½ lb (750 g) total weight

fresh flat-leaf parsley leaves, 2 tbsp

Two basic types of beans are grown, snap beans and shell beans. Snap beans, also known as green beans and runner beans, are eaten pod and all in quick and easy stir-fries, salads, and side dishes. Shell beans, such as cranberry beans and black-eyed peas, are "shelled" and used fresh or dried in soups, pastas, stews, and countless other dishes.

how to grow snap & shell beans

plant and maintain snap & shell beans

Snap and shell beans come in bush and pole varieties, and both thrive in full sun. The pole beans climb, climb, climb, so you need to provide them with a trellis, fence, tripod, or stakes. Plant seeds 1 inch (2.5 cm) deep and 4 inches (10 cm) apart in well-worked soil once night temperatures no longer drop below 55°F (13°C). For pole beans, install a trellis or other climbing structure in the soil before sowing the seeds, and space the seeds along the structure. You can also plant nursery starts, but because beans sprout so easily, it's more economical to grow them from seed.

You can start beans in small pots for staggered planting throughout the summer. Bush varieties are especially good candidates because they don't require trellising. They grow into easily managed tufts 2 feet (60 cm) high and can be tucked into the soil around tomato plants in a planter. Because beans have a short life span, you will need to plant them every 2 weeks throughout the growing season to ensure a steady supply. They can be grown in pots if space is limited. Water plants weekly and never let the soil dry out, or blossoms may drop. Fertilize the bean plants twice: once just after the plants leaf out and again when pods are beginning to form.

harvest snap & shell beans

Pick snap beans when they are young and tender and before the beans are bulging in the pod. The more you harvest, the more will grow. At the beginning of their production, bean plants are incredibly prolific. One small bush can yield about 1 lb (500 g) on a single picking—enough for a family of four. Green beans can be hard to see growing amid the green foliage and stems; purple and yellow varieties are easier to spot. Some experts recommend yanking the entire plant when harvesting, which can be heart-wrenching because it is full of blooms and baby beans, but makes sense toward the end of the plant's productive phase.

Shell beans can be harvested while still green, once the interior bean is rounded and mature. Or you can leave the pods on the plant until the outer skins are dry and brittle, then husk the dry beans and store them in jars. Beans that have been shelled while still green can either be cooked immediately, without soaking, or frozen for later use.

cherry tomato, green bean & wax bean salad with herbed bread crumbs

You can use any kind of snap bean in this salad, but I think it looks especially pretty made with dark green beans and pale yellow wax beans. Be sure to add a generous amount of salt to the boiling water so the beans stay vividly colored.

Bring a saucepan three-fourths full of salted water to a boil. Add the beans and cook until tender-crisp, about 3 minutes. Drain the beans and plunge into cold water to cool. Drain again.

Preheat the oven to 375°F (190°C). On a heavy rimmed baking sheet, toss the bread crumbs with 1½ tbsp of the olive oil, 1 tsp of the thyme, and 1 garlic clove. Sprinkle lightly with salt and toast in the oven, stirring occasionally, until golden brown, about 5 minutes. Remove from the oven and let cool.

In a large bowl, whisk together the remaining 2 tbsp olive oil, the vinegar, the remaining 2 tsp thyme, the remaining garlic clove, and ½ tsp salt. Add the reserved green and wax beans, cherry tomatoes, and red onion, season with pepper, and toss to combine. Stir in the bread crumbs. Transfer to a platter and serve.

kosher salt and freshly ground pepper

green beans, 6 oz (185 g), trimmed and cut into 3-inch (7.5-cm) lengths

yellow wax beans, 6 oz (185 g), trimmed and cut into 3-inch (7.5-cm) lengths

fresh bread crumbs from coarse country bread, 1½ cups (3 oz/90 g)

extra-virgin olive oil, 3½ tbsp

fresh thyme leaves, 3 tsp chopped

red wine vinegar, 2 tsp

garlic, 2 cloves, pressed

cherry tomatoes, 2 cups (12 oz/375 g), stemmed and halved

red onion, ½ cup chopped (2 oz/60 g)

spicy black-eyed pea salad with bacon

fresh black-eyed peas, 2 cups (12 oz/375 g) shelled

bay leaf, 1

fresh thyme sprigs, 2 large

applewood-smoked bacon, ¼ lb (125 g), cut into ¼-inch (6-mm) pieces

zucchini, 10 oz (315 g), trimmed and diced

red bell pepper, 1, seeded and diced

garlic, 2 large cloves, minced

jalapeño chile, 2 tbsp seeded and chopped

red wine vinegar, 1½ tbsp

green onions, 2, sliced

fresh cilantro leaves, 3 tbsp chopped

kosher salt and freshly ground pepper

MAKES 4 SERVINGS

Some markets carry packages of fully cooked or partially cooked fresh black-eyed peas. Use them if you are pressed for time or the peas are not yet in your garden or at the farmers' market. I like serving this great bean dish with barbecue.

Bring a large pot three-fourths full of water to a boil over high heat. Add the black-eyed peas, bay leaf, and thyme, reduce the heat to low, and cook until the peas are tender but still retain their shape, about 20 minutes. Drain the peas, discarding the bay leaf and thyme.

In a large, heavy frying pan over medium heat, fry the bacon until crisp, about 8 minutes. Using a slotted spoon, transfer the bacon pieces to paper towels to drain.

Pour off all but 2 tbsp of the bacon drippings from the pan and return the pan to medium-high heat. Add the zucchini, bell pepper, and garlic and sauté until the zucchini is almost tender, about 2 minutes. Add the drained peas and the chile and stir just until warm.

Transfer the pea mixture to a bowl and mix in the vinegar. Stir in the green onions, cilantro, and bacon. Season with salt and pepper and serve.

pork, green bean & eggplant stir-fry

You could fry up just about anything in Thai basil, ginger, and Sriracha and have it taste delicious, but pork, green beans and eggplant particularly shine here. The key to making this or any stir-fry successful is to have all the ingredients prepped before you start cooking. Chinese long beans can be used in place of the green beans if you like.

Using a sharp knife, cut the pork against the grain into slices ¼ inch (6 mm) thick. In a bowl, whisk together 2 tbsp of the soy sauce, 1 tbsp of the brown sugar, 1 tbsp water, 1 tbsp of the cornstarch, and 1 tsp of the Sriracha sauce until the sugar and cornstarch dissolve and the mixture is well blended. Add the pork and stir to coat with the marinade. Marinate the pork for 30 minutes at room temperature, or cover and let sit for up to 2 hours in the refrigerator.

In a small bowl, stir together 1 tbsp water and the remaining 1 tbsp soy sauce, 1 tbsp brown sugar, 1 tsp cornstarch, and 1 tsp Sriracha sauce until the sugar and cornstarch dissolve. Stir in the vinegar until well blended.

In a wok or a large, heavy frying pan over medium-high heat, warm 1 tbsp of the peanut oil and the sesame oil. When the oils are hot, add the green onions, garlic, and ginger and stir-fry until fragrant and just wilted, about 30 seconds. Add the green beans, eggplant, and bell pepper and stir-fry until the beans are tender-crisp, 4–6 minutes. Transfer the vegetables to a serving dish.

Add the remaining 1 tbsp peanut oil to the same pan over medium-high heat. When the oil is hot, add the pork with its marinade and stir-fry until the pork is no longer pink, about 4 minutes. Return the vegetable mixture to the pan and reserve the serving dish. Quickly stir the vinegar mixture to recombine and add to the pan along with the basil. Stir and toss until the pork and vegetables are lightly coated with the thickened sauce and the basil leaves are tender and wilted, about 1 minute. Transfer to the serving dish and serve with rice.

pork tenderloin, 1 lb (500 g)

soy sauce, 3 tbsp

golden brown sugar, 2 tbsp firmly packed

cornstarch, 1 tbsp plus 1 tsp

Sriracha sauce, 2 tsp

rice vinegar, 3 tbsp

peanut oil, 2 tbsp

Asian sesame oil, 1 tbsp

green onions, 2, sliced

garlic, 4 cloves, minced

fresh ginger, 1 tbsp peeled and minced

green beans, ¾ lb (375 g), trimmed and cut into 3-inch (7.5-cm) lengths

Asian eggplant, 1 small, sliced

red bell pepper, 1, seeded and sliced

fresh Thai or sweet basil leaves, ½ cup (½ oz/15 g)

steamed rice for serving

farro, corn & runner bean salad with goat cheese

kosher salt and freshly
ground pepper

farro, ½ cup (3 oz/90 g)

runner beans or green beans,
¾ lb (375 g), trimmed and
cut into 1½-inch (4-cm) lengths

yellow corn kernels, 2 cups
(12 oz/375 g), from about 2 ears

green onions, 3, thinly sliced

extra-virgin olive oil, 2 tbsp

fresh marjoram leaves, 1 tbsp
minced, plus 2 tsp whole leaves

white wine vinegar, 2 tbsp

garlic, 1 clove, pressed

Dijon mustard, 2 tsp

fresh goat cheese, ¼ lb (125 g),
crumbled

MAKES 4 SERVINGS

I'll make this dish on a summer day just to have it at the ready for lunch or dinner or an impromptu get-together. For a gorgeous presentation, I line the edge of a platter with sliced tomatoes and spoon the salad in the center.

Bring a large saucepan three-fourths full of salted water to a boil. Add the farro and boil until just tender, 25–30 minutes. Drain and let cool.

Refill the saucepan three-fourths full with salted water and bring to a boil. Add the beans and cook until tender-crisp, about 4 minutes. Drain and plunge into cold water to cool. Drain again.

In a large serving bowl, combine the farro, green beans, corn, and green onions. In a small bowl, muddle together the olive oil, minced marjoram, and ½ tsp salt. Whisk in the vinegar, garlic, and mustard. Pour the dressing over the salad and toss well. Season with salt and pepper, then sprinkle with the goat cheese and marjoram leaves and serve.

roasted snap beans with shallots & lemon

green beans, 6 oz (185 g),
trimmed

yellow wax beans, 6 oz (185 g),
trimmed

shallot, 3 tbsp thinly sliced

extra-virgin olive oil, 1 tbsp

lemon zest, 1 tsp grated

fresh lemon juice, 2–3 tsp

kosher salt and freshly
ground pepper

MAKES 4 SERVINGS

Preheat the oven to 400°F (200°C). On a large, heavy rimmed baking sheet, combine the beans, shallot, olive oil, and lemon zest and toss to mix well. Spread the beans out into a single layer.

Roast until the beans begin to brown, about 6 minutes. Stir and continue to roast until beans are tender and golden, about 6 minutes longer.

Remove from the oven, sprinkle with 2 tsp lemon juice, and stir to combine. Season lightly with salt and pepper, then taste and add salt, pepper, and lemon juice if needed. Transfer to a serving dish and serve hot or at room temperature.

Herbs are like fashion accessories. Just as the right belt or scarf can make an outfit, the right herb can make a meal. Herbs also accessorize the garden. Poked in around the vegetable plot, cascading out of pots, or treated as ornamentals in a grand planting, herbs shape, infuse, and color a garden, adding the perfect finishing touch.

how to grow summer herbs

plant and maintain basil

Easy to grow from seed or starts, basil, a relatively hardy annual, will even thrive in a pot on a windowsill. Plant seeds in well-dug soil in full sun after the weather is consistently warmer than 50°F (10°C), covering them with only about ½ inch (12 mm) of soil. Or plant indoors in cold climates and transplant seedlings when the sprouts have at least 4 leaves. As they grow, pinch off the top leaves to encourage a bushy profile. Remove any blossoms, too, to keep the basil from putting all its energy into making seeds. I recommend growing at least a dozen plants so you will have plenty to enjoy with tomatoes in summer and enough to make pesto at the end of the season.

plant and maintain lavender

This is not your standard culinary herb. The aromatic blossoms of lavender traditionally lend their perfume to colognes and potpourris and less commonly to food. American cooks add the blooms to their herbes de Provence blends, though French cooks do not. Different varieties of lavender are available, some of which thrive in dry, rocky environs, like Provence, and others that flourish in cooler climates, like England. Ask at your local nursery for the best type to grow in your area. In general, start from plants, not seeds, and provide well-drained, warm soil and full sun. In the coldest regions, put lavender in pots so you can follow the sun and then bring them indoors for the winter. In colder areas, make sure the soil dries out between waterings. Damp, soggy soil is lavender's number-one killer.

plant and maintain mint

A perennial, mint grows like a weed in my garden. It can get out of control easily, randomly sprouting up in planters, raised beds, and flowerpots. But come winter, it's gone, and I miss it terribly. Mint comes in several varieties, including standard spearmint and peppermint and the more exotic chocolate and pineapple mints. Buy plants at the nursery in spring, put them in the ground, and watch them take off. To keep them happy, give them partial shade and moist, modestly rich soil. They will die back in the winter, but return, usually with a vengeance, each spring. You can also grow mint from cuttings. Friends who are trying to tame their mint are usually a good source.

plant and maintain oregano

What would Italian, Greek, or Mexican food be without oregano? The primary types are Greek oregano, popular throughout the Mediterranean, and the more pungent Mexican oregano. Easy to grow from seed, start, or cutting, this perennial is as robust as mint, but not nearly as invasive, and produces pretty, low bushes. Grow in full sun in well-draining soil for a healthy crop. Pick sprigs frequently to encourage growth. Oregano will grow in even the coolest climates, though you will need to mulch plants in winter for protection in colder areas.

plant and maintain tarragon

Another hardy perennial, tarragon isn't fussy in the garden. It thrives in very cold climates and will even tolerate less-than-perfect soil, though it does appreciate good drainage. Buy plants in spring, choosing stronger-flavored French tarragon over Russian. Plants tend to die back in winter but will grow back in spring for a few years. If a plant thrives, divide it and plant it elsewhere in the garden or share it with a friend. If it struggles, replace it.

summer herb drizzle with sliced tomatoes & mozzarella

I make this aromatic condiment throughout the summer, varying the herbs and their amounts according to what is flourishing in the garden. I call it a "drizzle" because it's so good drizzled over tomatoes and mozzarella. It is also delicious on grilled vegetables, meats, fish, pizza—whatever could use a little herbal punch.

To make the drizzle, in a blender, combine the basil, parsley, oregano, thyme, summer savory, and garlic and pulse until finely chopped. With the blender running, slowly pour in the olive oil and process until smooth. Season with salt. Use immediately, or transfer the drizzle to a jar, cap tightly, and refrigerate for up to 1 week.

Arrange the tomato and mozzarella slices on a serving platter. Sprinkle with salt. Spoon about 3 tbsp of the herb drizzle over the tomatoes and mozzarella and serve.

for the summer herb drizzle

fresh basil leaves, ½ cup (½ oz/15 g)

fresh flat-leaf parsley leaves, ½ cup (½ oz/15 g)

fresh oregano and/or marjoram leaves, ⅓ cup (⅓ oz/10 g)

fresh thyme leaves, 3 tbsp

fresh summer savory leaves, 2 tbsp

garlic, 3 cloves

extra-virgin olive oil, 1 cup (8 fl oz/250 ml)

kosher salt

tomatoes, preferably heirloom, about 1½ lb (750 g), thickly sliced

fresh whole-milk mozzarella cheese, 1 lb (500 g), sliced

tarragon chicken salad

sour cream, 3 tbsp

Dijon mustard, 2 tbsp

mayonnaise, 2 tbsp

fresh tarragon, 2 tbsp chopped

honey, 2 tsp

pink peppercorns, 1 tsp chopped

cooked chicken, 2 cups
(12 oz/375 g) diced

celery, 2 ribs, thinly sliced

green onions, 2, thinly sliced

fresh flat-leaf parsley leaves,
2 tbsp chopped

kosher salt and freshly
ground pepper

MAKES 2–4 SERVINGS

This old-fashioned chicken salad makes a great no-cook summer dinner, whether spooned onto crisp lettuce leaves as a main-course salad or tucked between slices of toasted whole-grain bread for upscale chicken sandwiches.

In a bowl, whisk together the sour cream, mustard, mayonnaise, tarragon, honey, and pink peppercorns. Fold in the chicken, celery, green onions, and parsley. Season with salt and pepper. Serve.

dried summer herbs

select one of the following:

fresh mint sprigs

fresh oregano sprigs

fresh tarragon sprigs

fresh lavender sprigs

At the end of summer, I harvest fresh herbs and dry them for use the rest of the year. I harvest the basil, too, which I use to make pesto (page 117), because I feel the flavor is better preserved with olive oil and freezing than with drying.

To dry herbs, loosely tie a few branches together for each bunch. If you make the bunches too tight or too large, there will be too much leaf contact, which can cause rotting instead of drying. Tie a collar of waxed paper around each bunch to protect the leaves from dust, then hang the bunches in a cool, dry space until the leaves are dry, usually a couple of days. If you live in a moist climate, it may take a day or two longer.

When the leaves are dry, untie each bunch and gently crumble the leaves onto the waxed paper, removing only the blossoms for the lavender, and discard the stems. Using the paper as a guide, transfer each herb into a jar and seal tightly. Store in a cool cupboard for up to 4–6 months.

MAKES 6–8 SERVINGS

Adding a little mint to basil pesto gives the sauce a unique fresh flavor, but if you prefer a more traditional mix, omit the mint and use 2 cups (2 oz/60 g) basil. I make pesto at the end of the summer and freeze it for use throughout the winter.

To make the pesto, in a food processor, combine the basil, mint, pine nuts, cheese, and garlic and pulse until finely chopped. Add the oil and pulse until a coarse purée forms. Season with salt. Use right away, or transfer to a container, press plastic wrap directly onto the surface of the pesto, cover, and refrigerate for up to 4 days or freeze for up to 4 months.

To cook the pasta, bring a pot of water to a rapid boil and salt generously. Add the pasta, stir, and cook until al dente, about 8 minutes or according to the package directions. While the pasta is cooking, in a saucepan over high heat, bring the cream just to a boil. Remove from the heat, whisk in the pesto, and season with salt and pepper. Drain the pasta and transfer to a serving bowl. Pour the sauce over the pasta, toss well, and serve.

pasta with basil & mint pesto

for the pesto

fresh basil leaves, 1½ cups (1½ oz/45 g)

fresh mint leaves, ½ cup (½ oz/15 g)

pine nuts, ½ cup (2½ oz/75 g), toasted (page 217)

Parmesan cheese, ½ cup (2 oz/60 g) grated, plus more for serving

garlic, 3 cloves, chopped

extra-virgin olive oil, ⅓ cup (3 fl oz/80 ml)

kosher salt and ground pepper

dried linguine, 1 lb (500 g)

heavy cream, 1 cup (8 fl oz/250 ml)

MAKES 6–8 SERVINGS

I make this refreshing iced tea, with its cooling mint and clean cucumber flavor, with decaffeinated green tea so I can sip it all day long when the weather is hot.

In a large heatproof pitcher, combine the tea bags, 12 of the mint sprigs, and the lavender. Pour in the water and let steep for 8 minutes. Remove the tea bags and let the tea cool to room temperature. Add the cucumber and lemon, cover, and refrigerate for at least 1 hour or preferably overnight.

Taste the tea and sweeten with a little honey, if desired, stirring until the honey dissolves. Fill tall glasses with ice cubes, and strain the tea into the glasses. Garnish each glass with a mint sprig and serve.

herb-infused tea with cucumber, lavender & mint

green tea bags, 5

fresh mint sprigs, 18–20 small

fresh whole lavender blossoms, 3, or ½ tsp dried

boiling water, 8 cups (64 fl oz/2 l)

cucumber, 1, sliced

lemon, 1, cut into 8 rounds

honey (optional)

ice cubes, for serving

The sunny days of summer deliver a bounty of juicy fruits: berries, cherries, plums, apricots, peaches. Whether they are enjoyed out of hand, cut for salads, baked into pies and crisps, arranged atop pastry cream–lined tartlets, simmered for jam, or churned into ice cream, nothing tastes more like summertime than garden-fresh fruits.

how to grow
berries & stone fruits

plant and maintain raspberries and blackberries

Known as bramble plants or cane berries, raspberries and blackberries can be grown in all but the coldest climates. The plants, known as canes because they resemble bare, thorny sticks with a few roots attached, are available from nurseries and mail-order sources. Plant the canes in full sun in good-draining sandy loam, preferably on a gently sloping hillside, when dormant: early winter in warmer climes and after danger of frost in colder areas. Although both berries will grow well in partial shade, the more sun the plants get, the more berries you will get. Space raspberry plants about 3 feet (1 m) apart, and blackberries 5 to 6 feet (1.5 to 2 m) apart. Harvest the berries as they ripen. After the last harvest, cut raspberry brambles back to a 6-inch (15-cm) cane, and cut blackberries back to the ground.

plant and maintain blueberries

Easy to grow, blueberry plants are hardy deciduous shrubs that thrive in full sun and rich, sandy, well-draining soil. A blueberry variety suitable to almost every climate exists, even my Southern California one. If you lack the best soil conditions, you can plant blueberries in raised beds or even in large containers. Space them about 3 feet (1 m) apart if you'd like your plants to grow into a hedge, and about 4 to 5 feet (1.25 to 1.5 m) apart for separates shrubs. Keep blueberry plants well watered and well weeded. Remove the blossoms the first year to encourage plant and root health and a higher yield the following year. Remove dead branches and twiggy growth in early spring. When the berries are ripe, harvest them right away, before the birds do.

plant and maintain stone fruits

Apricot, cherry, nectarine, peach, and plum trees make pretty additions to the garden: they bloom colorfully in the spring, leaf out and fruit in the summer, provide a little fall color, and become dramatically bare in winter. Most stone-fruit varieties require "chilling hours" to bear fruit, so if you live in a warmer zone, be sure to select trees that require less than 500 hours below 45°F (7°C). Purchase bare root, rather than potted, trees, for planting. The selection is bigger, they are easier to transport, and they have a lower price tag. Check if the tree is self-pollinating; if not, you will need to plant at least two trees.

Select a flat, sunny spot in your garden, and plant trees at least 12 feet (4 m) apart. Or plant two or three different varieties close together (about 12 inches/30 cm) and allow the trees to grow as one. Feed the trees annually and prune judiciously in winter. The trees will begin to bear fruit 2 years after planting.

Apricot trees fruit on the second-year growth, so prune only every other year after harvest. Plums are a great choice for most gardens because so many varieties are available that you are sure to find one that will flourish in your climate. The self-pollinating Santa Rosa is my personal favorite. Sour cherry varieties are also self-pollinating, and cherry trees are the least fussy at pruning time.

grilled pork tenderloin with apricot chutney

for the apricot chutney

coriander seeds, 1 tbsp

shallot, ¼ cup (1 oz/30 g) sliced

golden brown sugar, 2 tbsp packed

cider vinegar, 1 tbsp

cinnamon stick, 1

árbol chile, 1 or 1 small pinch crushed red pepper flakes

apricots, 1½ lb (750 g), pitted and diced or 1½ lb (750 g) peaches, peeled, pitted, and diced

honey, 1 tbsp

kosher salt, ¼ tsp

fresh cilantro leaves, 2 tbsp chopped

fresh mint leaves, 2 tbsp chopped

pork tenderloin, 1, about 1¼ lb (625 g)

Asian sesame oil, 1 tbsp

coriander seeds, 1 tbsp

kosher salt, ½ tsp

honey, 1½ tbsp

MAKES 6 SERVINGS

At a backyard get-together, I like to serve this pork hot off the grill, but it's also delicious thinly sliced and served cold at a picnic. In both cases, the sweet-tart apricot chutney is the perfect partner. If you like, substitute peaches or plums.

To make the chutney, in a small frying pan over medium heat, lightly toast the coriander seeds, about 1 minute. Set aside.

In a saucepan over medium heat, combine the shallot, brown sugar, vinegar, cinnamon stick, chile, and 2 tbsp water, bring to a simmer, and simmer until the shallot is tender and the mixture is syrupy, about 2 minutes. Stir in the apricots and toasted coriander seeds and cook until the apricots are just tender, about 3 minutes. Remove from the heat and stir in the honey and kosher salt. Let cool completely and stir in the cilantro and mint.

Prepare a medium-hot fire for direct-heat cooking in a charcoal or gas grill. Lightly crush the coriander seeds. Brush the pork on all sides with the sesame oil, then coat evenly with the crushed coriander seeds and salt. Place the pork directly over the fire and grill, turning frequently, until well browned on all sides, about 12 minutes total.

Spread the honey over the pork and continue to grill until an instant-read thermometer inserted into the thickest part of the tenderloin registers 140°F (60°C) and the pork is nicely glazed, about 4 minutes longer. Transfer the pork to a platter, let it rest for 5 minutes, then cut into thin slices and serve with the chutney.

Use slightly firm fruit for this rustic tart. Plums are not freestone fruits, which means the flesh does not separate easily from the pit. To make uniform slices, I cut off the flesh in halves, positioning the knife close to either side of the pit, then I cut the halves into wedges. You can substitute Pluots or Apriums, if desired.

In a bowl, toss together the plums, granulated sugar, flour, and salt. Let the plums stand while you roll out the dough.

Preheat the oven to 400°F (200°C). On a large, lightly floured sheet of parchment paper, roll out the dough into a round 13 inches (33 cm) in diameter. Slide the parchment paper with the dough round onto a heavy rimmed baking sheet.

Scatter the almond paste pieces evenly over the center of the dough round, leaving a 2-inch (5-cm) border of dough uncovered. Using a slotted spoon, distribute the plums evenly over the almond paste, again leaving the border uncovered. Reserve any juices in the bowl. Using the parchment paper as an aid, fold the uncovered border of dough up over the plums, pleating as needed and pressing gently to secure in place.

Brush the dough border lightly with the egg white, and sprinkle the turbinado sugar over the egg white. Drizzle any reserved juices from the bowl over the plums. Dot the plums with the butter. Bake until the crust is golden brown and the juices bubble in the center, about 50 minutes.

Remove from the oven and let cool slightly on the baking sheet on a wire rack. Slide the croustade and parchment onto a flat platter. Serve warm.

plum-almond croustade

plums, 1¼ lb (625 g), pitted and cut into wedges ½ inch (12 mm) thick

granulated sugar, ¼ cup (2 oz/60 g)

unbleached all-purpose flour, 2 tsp

kosher salt, pinch

savory pastry dough (page 215)

almond paste, ¼ lb (125 g), broken into ½-inch (12-mm) pieces

large egg white, 1, lightly beaten

turbinado sugar, 2 tbsp

unsalted butter, 1 tbsp, cut into small pieces

peach ice cream

peaches, 1 lb (500 g), pitted and chopped

sugar, ¾ cup (6 oz/185 g)

citric acid, ½ tsp

heavy cream, 1¼ cups (10 fl oz/310 ml)

large egg yolks, 6

pure vanilla extract, 1 tsp

MAKES ABOUT 1 QT (1 L)

Fresh peach ice cream is my signature summer dessert. I leave the skins on because they add lovely color and pure peach flavor. The citric acid keeps the peaches from turning brown. Look for it at cake-supply stores.

In a large bowl, combine the peaches, ½ cup (4 oz/125 g) of the sugar, and the citric acid. Stir and mash the peaches gently with the back of a spoon.

In a heavy saucepan over medium heat, bring the cream to a gentle boil. Whisk together the egg yolks and the remaining ¼ cup (2 oz/60 g) sugar until blended. Remove the cream from the heat and gradually whisk it into the egg mixture. Return the mixture to the pan and stir constantly over low heat until the custard thickens enough to coat the back of the spoon, about 8 minutes. Do not boil. Strain the custard through a fine-mesh sieve into a bowl and let cool until just warm. Whisk the custard into the peach mixture, then stir in the vanilla. Transfer the custard to an ice-cream maker and freeze according to the manufacturer's directions. Serve right away, or store in an airtight container in the freezer for up to 2 weeks.

honey-roasted peaches with vanilla cream

unsalted butter, 2 tbsp, cut into 12 small pieces, plus melted butter for baking dish

golden brown sugar, ¼ cup (2 oz/60 g) firmly packed

vanilla bean, 2-inch (5-cm) piece, split lengthwise

peaches, 6 small ripe (about 1½ lb/750 g), halved and pitted

honey, 4 tbsp (3 oz/90 g)

vanilla whipped cream (page 217)

fresh thyme leaves, for garnish

MAKES 6 SERVINGS

Preheat the oven to 400°F (200°C). Line a large baking pan with aluminum foil, and brush the foil with melted butter.

Put the brown sugar in a bowl. Using the tip of a small knife, scrape the seeds from the vanilla bean into the brown sugar, then stir to mix well. Arrange the peaches, skin side down, in a single layer in the prepared pan. Drizzle the peaches evenly with 2 tbsp of the honey, and sprinkle evenly with the brown sugar. Dot the peaches with the butter.

Roast the peaches until they are tender and browned, about 20 minutes. Divide the peaches halves among serving dishes. Drizzle the peaches evenly with any syrup remaining in the pan, then drizzle each serving with honey. Top each with whipped cream, sprinkle with thyme, and serve.

You can use any combination of berries in these prettier-than-pastry-shop tartlets that are surprisingly easy to make. I use a "no roll" crust, a pastry cream that can be made days in advance, and a little jam (the Lemon-Kissed Strawberry Jam, page 68, is lovely here) to sweeten and glaze the berries.

In a bowl, stir together the pastry cream and sour cream to loosen. In another bowl, whisk together the jam and liqueur to blend.

Gently fold the berries into the jam mixture until coated. Divide the cream evenly among the tartlet shells, spreading it evenly, then top with the berries, dividing evenly. Remove the tartlets from the pans and serve.

berry-cream tartlets

pastry cream (page 217)

sour cream, 2 tbsp

berry jam such as raspberry, boysenberry, or strawberry, 2 tbsp

berry liqueur such as framboise, 1 tbsp

mixed berries, 2 cups (8 oz/250 g), stemmed and cored if using strawberries

fully baked tartlet shells from sweet pastry dough (page 215), 4

MAKES 3 HALF-PT (8 FL OZ/250 ML EACH) JARS

Santa Rosa plums have dark purple skin and intensely flavored red flesh. The fruit that I don't eat directly off the tree, I simmer into my favorite jam.

Put the plums in a heavy saucepan, cover, place over low heat, and cook until the plums are very soft and juicy, about 30 minutes. Remove from the heat, let cool slightly, and remove and discard the pits.

Return the plums to medium heat and simmer, uncovered, until slightly thickened and reduced to about 2⅔ cups (26 oz/780 g), about 7 minutes. Add the sugar, stir, and boil gently over medium heat, stirring constantly, until slightly thickened and reduced to about 3 cups (30 oz/940 g), about 4 minutes.

Transfer the jam to clean jars, cap tightly, and refrigerate. It will keep in the refrigerator for up to 2 weeks.

santa rosa plum jam

Santa Rosa plums, 2 lb (1 kg)

sugar, 2 cups (1 lb/500 g)

FALL & WINTER

kale lacinato, dwarf blue curled • **chard** bright lights, rhubarb
mustard greens red giant, mizuna, green wave • **collard greens**
champion, flash, vates • **carrots** bolero nantes, little sweet, thumbelina,
purple haze, red samurai, white satin • **beets** golden, red sangria,
striped chioggia, bulls blood • **sweet potatoes** centennial, jewel
winter squashes & pumpkins honey bear acorn squash, butternut
waltham, kabocha, rouge vif d'etamps • **rosemary** blue boy, blue spires,
gorizia • **sage** holt's mammouth, icterina, tricolor • **thyme** common,
silver, lemon, lime • **citrus** bearss lime, mexican lime, moro blood
orange, midknight valencia orange, cara cara orange, shasta or
yosemite gold mandarin, clementine mandarin, goldnugget mandarin,
improved meyer lemon, oroblanco grapefruit, rio red grapefruit
apples rubinette, newtown pippin, zestar • **pears** comice, seckel, orcas

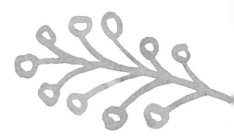

FALL & WINTER

Depending on your climate, fall and winter can be a time of abundant harvests of root vegetables such as carrots, beets, and potatoes; tangy-sweet citrus, crisp apples, and juicy pears; hard-skinned squashes; and leafy, deep emerald kale, chard, and other greens. Or it can be a period when much of your land lies fallow. In warmer zones, the planting area must be quickly rebooted so that it can transition smoothly from summer vegetables to fall plantings. Less activity takes place in cold climates, but the garden still requires attention as it heads into the dormant season.

The kitchen remains busy regardless of whether it's icy cold or relatively mild outdoors, with such cool-weather comfort foods as hearty soups, pastas, braised greens, and roasted root vegetables filling daily menus. Sweets make a good showing, too, with citrus fruits turned into silky smooth curds and icy granitas, apples sautéed or baked into cakes, and pears poached and doused with bittersweet chocolate–honey sauce.

what to do in colder climates

Start the fall chores in cooler climates by harvesting any remaining fruit and vegetables before the first hard freeze. If a frost hits unexpectedly, harvest as soon as possible after it and eat what you gather right away, as it will spoil quickly.

Apply a protective layer of mulch to perennials, such as berries, asparagus, and strawberries. If you have carrots and cauliflower that you plan to overwinter in the garden, mark the carrots with a layer of mulch and blanch the cauliflower by folding the leaves over the crown. Feed all overwintering plants with a low-nitrogen, high-phosphorus, high-potassium fertilizer to help them become cold hardy.

When bringing your potted herbs inside for the winter, keep in mind that your indoor "climate" is much drier than what the herbs knew outdoors. Take care of your potted plants by misting them frequently with water.

what to do in warmer climates

In warm growing zones, it's time to get busy. If you plan on growing vegetables throughout the fall and winter after reaping summer's bounty, your soil will need special attention. Nourishing summer's harvest of tomatoes, zucchini, cucumbers, and green beans has leeched a lot of good stuff from the earth. Think of all that colorful produce in terms of nutrients in the soil—nutrients that need to be replaced. A fall crop planted without amending the soil would fail to thrive.

First, remove any spent plants along with any roots from nearby trees that might have intruded in a search for water over the long, hot summer. The end of the season is usually a hot, dry time for your dirt. Take care to moisten the soil by watering it in. "Watering in" means to soak the raised bed on a daily basis until the soil is evenly moist. This process can take up to a week if the bed has been sitting fallow and unwatered since September.

The soil will once again need digging and double digging with added amendments of compost and organic fertilizer. All this soil preparation may seem like a heap of trouble, but you don't want to miss out on this wonderful cool growing season.

a note about fruit trees

Fruit trees are dormant in the winter in warm and cold zones. In both areas, leaves and any pieces of rotten fruit should be cleared from under the trees and composted. Remove any stakes and provide trunk protectors if you suspect rodent damage. Late winter is the optimal time to prune. If necessary, consult an expert for the best way to proceed to ensure good yields in the future.

Doctors routinely advise us to eat more leafy green vegetables, because they are rich in vitamins A, K, and C and are a great source of fiber. It is an easy prescription to follow. Greens demand relatively little attention in the garden and are versatile in the kitchen, where they can be combined with sausage in pasta, simmered in a hearty soup, or braised with onions and bacon.

how to grow greens

plant and maintain kale

A popular green related to cabbage, kale comes in many appealing varieties: Russian, curly, red, flowering, and lacinato (aka dinosaur and cavolo nero). It thrives in colder climates. In fact, plants grown in fall will survive snow and actually improve, or "sweeten," in flavor when picked after a frost. In my warmer zone, I like to grow lacinato kale in successive plantings throughout the late fall and winter. Sow seeds ½ inch (12 mm) apart in rich, well-draining soil and water and fertilize regularly. As the kale grows, pick off leaves as needed. The plant will continue to grow and produce more leaves for months.

plant and maintain chard

Another green that keeps on giving, chard plants can be harvested for well over a year. This abundance, combined with the beauty of the red and rainbow varieties, makes Swiss chard a must for any vegetable patch. Sow seeds as you do for kale. In warmer areas, plant in the fall to enjoy all winter and into the spring. In cooler areas, plant about 1 month before the last predicted frost and continue to harvest leaves until snow falls. Sow seeds ½ inch (12 mm) deep and 2 inches (5 cm) apart in 18-inch (45-cm) rows. After sprouting, thin seedlings to about 12 inches (30 cm) apart. Keep the soil moist and fertilize with a 10-10-10 blend when plants are established and then a month or two after that. Harvest leaves as you need them.

plant and maintain mustard greens

Two of my favorite spicy mustard types are feathery-shaped mizuna and red mustard. Sow seeds ½ inch (12 mm) deep in well-draining soil, and thin seedlings to about 6 inches (15 cm) apart. If the plants get plenty of water, full sun, and low temperatures, they will produce tender leaves that are great eaten raw in salads when small or cooked when larger. Too much warm weather can make the leaves tough and overly spicy, like strong Dijon mustard.

plant and maintain collard greens

The collard plant looks a little different than most greens. It has a thick, tall center stem and large leaves that can be harvested as the plant grows. Grow collard greens from seed or starts spaced about 12 inches (30 cm) apart. In colder areas, plant in early spring for harvest in the summer, fall, and winter. Certain varieties, such as Morris Heading, "sweeten" after being exposed to frost. In warmer areas, plant in the fall for winter and spring harvest.

radicchio & kale salad with pancetta

extra-virgin olive oil, 2 tbsp

balsamic vinegar, 1 tbsp

fresh lemon juice, 1 tbsp

garlic, 1 clove, pressed

kosher salt, ¼ tsp

lacinato or other kale, 1 bunch (about 1 lb/500 g)

radicchio, 1 small head, torn into small pieces

pancetta, 3 thin slices (1½ oz/45 g)

Pecorino Romano cheese, ¼ cup (1½ oz) grated

freshly ground pepper

MAKES 4 SERVINGS

Kale salads are strangely addictive for something so darned good for us. But lest we feast on something too virtuous, this flavorful version features salty bits of pancetta and cheese.

In a large bowl, whisk together the oil, vinegar, lemon juice, garlic and salt. Using a sharp knife, remove the center ribs from the kale leaves and discard. Stack the leaves, roll them into a cylinder, and cut crosswise into strips. Add the kale and radicchio and toss until well coated. Cover and refrigerate until the kale is wilted and tender, about 4 hours.

In a large, heavy frying pan over medium heat, fry the pancetta until crisp, turning once, about 8 minutes. Transfer the pancetta to a plate to cool, then crumble over the salad. Add the cheese, season with pepper, then toss to combine. Serve.

white bean & kale soup

dried cannellini beans, 1 cup (7 oz/220 g)

extra-virgin olive oil, 2 tbsp

yellow onions, 2, chopped

garlic, 8 cloves, chopped

fresh rosemary, 1 tbsp chopped

red pepper flakes, ½ tsp

chicken broth, 8–9 cups (2–2.1 l)

kale, 10 oz (315 g), ribs removed and leaves chopped into 1-inch (2.5-cm) pieces

kosher salt and freshly ground pepper

MAKES 4 SERVINGS

Pick over the beans, place in a bowl, add water to cover by 2 inches (5 cm), and let soak overnight. The next day, in a large, heavy pot over medium heat, warm the olive oil. Add the onions and sauté until golden brown and tender, about 10 minutes. Stir in the garlic, rosemary, and red pepper flakes and cook, stirring, for 1 minute.

Drain the beans, add to the pot along with 8 cups (64 fl oz/2 l) of the broth, and bring to a simmer. Reduce the heat to medium-low, cover partially, and simmer until the beans are very tender yet still retain their shape, about 1½ hours. Stir in the kale and simmer until the kale is very tender, about 20 minutes. Season with salt and pepper and add additional broth if necessary to thin. Ladle the soup into warmed bowls and serve.

barley with kale & lemon

kosher salt

pearl barley, ½ cup (3½ oz/105 g)

lacinato kale, 1 bunch
(about 1 lb/500 g)

extra-virgin olive oil, 2 tbsp

yellow onion, 1 small,
finely chopped

garlic, 4 cloves, chopped

red pepper flakes, ¼ tsp

grated lemon zest, ½ tsp

fresh lemon juice, 1–2 tbsp

Barley is often an overlooked grain, and while it might not be as sexy as its Italian cousin farro, it is far more accessible and just as satisfying. Blended with kale, you have a versatile dish that is perfect alongside sausages or roasted meats, or served as a vegetarian main course.

Bring a large saucepan half full of salted water to a boil over high heat. Add the barley and cook until tender, about 45 minutes. Drain and set aside.

Meanwhile, using a sharp knife, remove the center ribs from the kale leaves and discard. Stack the leaves, roll them into a cylinder, and cut crosswise into thin strips.

In a large, heavy frying over medium-high heat, warm the olive oil. Add the onion and sauté until golden brown, about 6 minutes. Add the garlic and sauté until fragrant, about 1 minute. Reduce the heat to medium, add the kale, and sprinkle with the red pepper flakes. Sauté until the kale is tender and wilted, about 7 minutes.

Stir in the lemon zest and season with salt, then add the lemon juice to taste. Transfer to a warmed serving dish and serve.

Pimentón de la Vera, a smoked paprika from western Spain, boosts the smoky flavor of the bacon in this pot of tender greens. Serve the greens with eggs and grits for brunch or with roast chicken or pork for dinner, or, if you're like me, you might just whip up a batch of these greens for a much-needed snack after tending the garden—the perfect reward.

In a large, heavy pot over medium heat, fry the bacon until crisp, about 8 minutes. Using a slotted spoon, transfer the bacon pieces to a plate. Add the onion to the drippings in the pan and sauté until golden brown and tender, about 8 minutes. Stir in the garlic and saute until fragrant, about 1 minute. Add the paprika and stir until fragrant, about 1 minute.

Add half of the greens and stir until wilted, about 4 minutes. Add the remaining greens and stir until wilted, about 3 minutes more. Pour in the broth and deglaze the pan, stirring to scrape up any browned bits on the pan bottom. Cook until the greens are very tender and the liquid evaporates slightly, about 10 minutes. Transfer to a warmed serving dish and serve.

braised greens with bacon & smoked paprika

applewood-smoked bacon, ¼ lb (125 g), cut into ½-inch (12-mm) pieces

yellow onion, 1, chopped

garlic, 4 cloves, chopped

smoked paprika, 1 tbsp

mixed greens such as collard and mustard, 1 lb (500 g), torn into pieces

chicken broth, ½ cup (4 fl oz/125 ml)

penne with chard & sausage

This is one of those great pasta dishes that tastes like it was slaved over for days but comes together in under 30 minutes. You can use other greens from your garden in place of the chard. Just make sure you cook them until they are tender.

In a large, deep frying pan over medium-high heat, fry the sausage meat, breaking it up with the back of a spoon, until well browned and crusty, about 8 minutes. Using a slotted spoon, transfer the sausage to a bowl.

Return the pan to medium-high heat, add the onion, and sauté until golden brown and tender, about 5 minutes. Add the garlic and stir for 1 minute. Pour in the wine and deglaze the pan, scraping up any browned bits from the pan bottom, then cook until the wine evaporates. Add the chard and cook, stirring, until it is wilted and tender, about 5 minutes.

Meanwhile, to cook the pasta, bring a large pot of water to a rapid boil and salt generously. Add the pasta, stir well, and cook until about 1 minute shy of al dente, about 9 minutes or according to package directions.

Drain the pasta, reserving 1 cup (8 fl oz/250 ml) of the cooking water, and add the pasta to the frying pan along with the sausage. Reduce the heat to medium and cook, stirring, until blended. Add ½ cup (4 fl oz/125 ml) of the cooking water and stir until the pasta is nicely coated with the sauce, about 2 minutes. Stir in the Parmesan and season with salt and pepper. Add a little more of the cooking water if needed to moisten the pasta.

Serve in warmed shallow bowls. Pass additional cheese at the table.

hot Italian sausages, ¾ lb (375 g), casings removed

yellow onion, 1, chopped

garlic, 6 cloves, chopped

dry white wine, ¼ cup (2 fl oz/60 ml)

Swiss chard, 1 lb (500 g), ribs removed and leaves cut into wide strips

penne, ½ lb (250 g)

kosher salt and freshly ground pepper

Parmesan cheese, ¼ cup (1 oz/30 g) grated, plus more for serving

If you don't like beets, you have probably never eaten a sweet, just-yanked beet from a backyard garden. The same is true for all the vegetables here. That's because if you grow roots and tubers yourself, you can harvest them when they are still small and tender and then showcase their youthful flavors and textures in scores of simple dishes.

how to grow roots & tubers

plant and maintain carrots

Carrots like rich soil that is a little loose and sandy, so the long, narrow root can grow deep. Carrot seeds are so tiny that you may want to mix them with a little sand to make sowing easier. Plant the seeds ¼ inch (6 mm) deep and 1 to 2 inches (2.5 to 5 cm) apart in rows about 12 inches (30 cm) apart. After the carrots have sprouted, thin them to about 3 inches (7.5 cm) apart. Pull them when they are the size you want. If you decide to overwinter the carrots in the ground, cover them with mulch. The tops will die back, so keep the area marked. They will taste great all winter long, but harvest them before spring, because if left in the ground too long, their flavor will diminish.

plant and maintain beets

Like carrots, beets are grown from seed. Sow beet seeds (they are large and easy to handle) in rich, well-tilled, good-draining soil about 1½ inches (4 cm) deep and 2 inches (5 cm) apart in rows about 12 inches (30 cm) apart. When the sprouts are about 2 inches (5 cm) tall, thin them to 3 to 4 inches (7.5 to 10 cm) apart for good root development, saving the sprouts for a salad. Water regularly to prevent the roots from cracking. In colder climates, plant beets in the late summer for fall harvest, or in early spring for a summer harvest. Beets tend to bolt if exposed to too much heat, so if you live in a warm zone, look for heat-tolerant varieties.

plant and maintain sweet potatoes

Sweet potato starts, known as slips, are small rooted pieces of the tuber, and you can grow your own slips from a healthy, organic sweet potato. Cut 2 inches (5 cm) off the end of a sweet potato, then secure 3 toothpicks in the side of the sweet potato at even intervals. Fill a jar with water, position the sweet potato so that the bottom 1 inch (2.5 cm) of it is in the water, and place the jar on a sunny windowsill. Allow the sweet potato to root and sprout. When the sprouts are about 5 inches (13 cm) tall, cut them from the potato and plant in potting soil in small pots. When the slips have developed a healthy root, they are ready to plant in the garden in a sunny spot. Plant them in spring about 4 inches (10 cm) deep and 8 inches (20 cm) apart. The foliage is pleasing to the eye, so I position a climbing cage among the slips. Sweet potatoes can take up to 150 days to mature, but be sure to harvest them before the first frost. Dig up tubers carefully to avoid cutting and bruising your yield. Sweet potatoes can be eaten just after harvesting but their flavor improves when they are cured for a week or two. After unearthing, allow sweet potatoes to dry in the sun, then brush off the dirt and cure in a warm, humid area. Store in a cool, dark place.

pickled carrots with fennel & bay

baby carrots, 1 lb (500 g)

kosher salt, 3 tbsp

fennel seeds, 1 rounded tbsp

cider vinegar, 1 cup
(8 fl oz/250 ml)

sugar, ¼ cup (2 oz/60 g)

garlic, 2 cloves, thinly sliced

bay leaves, 4, preferably fresh

red pepper flakes, ¼ tsp

I love the way the sweetness of fennel and bay leaves play off the sweetness of carrots here. I make these crisp-crunchy pickles with the wee carrots that I grow or find at the farmers' market, but you could always cut larger carrots into sticks.

Trim and lightly peel the carrots. Fill a saucepan with water, add 1½ tbsp of the salt, and bring to a boil. Add the carrots, return to a boil, and boil for 1 minute. Drain the carrots and divide them evenly between two 1-pt (16–fl oz/500-ml) jars with tightly fitting lids, standing the carrots on end.

In a heavy frying pan over medium heat, toast the fennel seeds, shaking the pan often, until lightly browned and fragrant, about 30 seconds. Transfer the seeds to a saucepan and add 1½ cups (12 fl oz/375 ml) water, the vinegar, sugar, garlic, bay leaves, red pepper flakes, and the remaining 1½ tbsp salt. Place over medium heat and bring slowly to a boil, allowing the flavors to blend.

Using a ladle, spoon the brine over the carrots, dividing the bay leaves, garlic, and fennel seeds evenly between the jars. Let cool completely uncovered, then cap the jars tightly and refrigerate overnight before serving. The carrots will keep in the refrigerator for up to 3 weeks.

roasted beets with farro & blue cheese

beets, 8 small

extra-virgin olive oil, 4 tbsp
(2 fl oz/60 ml), plus more
for drizzling

kosher salt

farro, 1½ cups (7 oz/220 g)

red wine vinegar, 2 tbsp

garlic, 1 clove, pressed

radicchio, 1 small head, quartered
and thinly sliced crosswise

green onions, ½ cup (1½ oz/45 g)
thinly sliced

fresh flat-leaf parsley leaves,
⅓ cup (⅓ oz/10 g)

blue cheese, ¼ lb (125 g),
crumbled

MAKES 6—8 SERVINGS

In this hearty grain salad, farro, an ancient Italian wheat strain with a chewy texture and a nutty whole-grain flavor, takes on the pink hue of the beets. The appearance may seem a bit girlish, but I can assure you that everyone I've served this to loves it, especially if they have helped to plant or harvest the beets. Radicchio adds a subtly bitter counterpoint to the sweet, earthy beets.

Preheat the oven to 350°F (180°C). Cut off the beet tops and reserve for another use. Place the beets in a single layer in a heavy ovenproof frying pan just large enough to accommodate them, and drizzle with olive oil. Cover with aluminum foil. Roast the beets until tender when pierced with a small, sharp knife, about 40 minutes. Let cool completely.

While the beets are roasting, bring a large saucepan three-fourths full of salted water to a boil over hight heat. Add the farro. Reduce the heat to medium and cook until just tender, 25–30 minutes. Drain the farro and transfer to a large bowl. Immediately stir in 2 tbsp of the olive oil, 1 tbsp of the vinegar, and the garlic. Let cool to room temperature.

Peel and trim the beets, then cut each beet into 6 to 8 wedges. Add to the farro along with the radicchio, green onions, and parsley and stir to combine.

In a small bowl, whisk together the remaining 2 tbsp olive oil and the remaining 1 tbsp vinegar. Drizzle the dressing evenly over the salad, add the blue cheese, toss well, and serve.

MAKES 4 SERVINGS

Preheat the oven to 350°F (180°C). Cut off the beet tops and reserve for another use. Place the beets in a single layer in a baking dish just large enough to accommodate them, and drizzle with vegetable oil. Cover with aluminum foil. Roast the beets until tender when pierced with a small, sharp knife, about 40 minutes. Let cool completely.

Meanwhile, trim the fennel bulb, reserving the fronds for garnish, and thinly slice it crosswise. Peel and trim the beets, then slice and arrange in a single layer on a platter. Top the beets with the fennel, then the tangerine segments, and finally the avocado slices.

In a small bowl, whisk together the vinegar, shallot, garlic, and 2 tbsp of the tangerine juice. Whisk in the olive oil and season with salt. Pour the vinaigrette over the salad and season with pepper. Serve.

roasted beet, avocado & fennel salad with tangerine vinaigrette

beets, 6 small

vegetable oil, for drizzling

fennel bulb, 1 small

tangerines, 3, 2 cut into segments (page 217) and 1 juiced

avocado, 1, halved, pitted, peeled, and sliced

white balsamic vinegar, 2 tbsp

shallot, 2 tbsp minced

garlic, 1 clove, pressed

extra-virgin olive oil, 2 tbsp

kosher salt and freshly ground pepper

MAKES 4 SERVINGS

Homegrown sweet potatoes tend to be smaller than store-bought, so if you don't dig up your own, look for small ones at the market. Make sure the butter is quite soft before you mix in the lime juice so the juice is fully incorporated.

Preheat the oven to 425°F (220°C). Pierce the unpeeled sweet potatoes in a few spots with a small, sharp knife and place on a rimmed baking sheet. Bake until tender when pierced with a fork, about 50 minutes.

While the sweet potatoes are baking, in a small bowl, stir together the butter, chile powder, lime juice, honey, lime zest, and salt until well blended.

When the sweet potatoes are ready, remove from the oven, slit each sweet potato lengthwise down the center to open, then place on individual plates. Top the sweet potatoes with the flavored butter, dividing it evenly, and serve.

baked sweet potatoes with chile-lime butter

orange-fleshed sweet potatoes, 4, about 6 oz (185 g) each

unsalted butter, 4 tbsp (2 oz/60 g), at room temperature

ancho chile powder, 1 tbsp

fresh lime juice, 1 tbsp

honey, 1 tsp

lime zest, ¼ tsp grated

kosher salt, ¼ tsp

roasted beets with toasted pecans & greens

beets, 6 small

extra-virgin olive oil, 2 tbsp plus more for drizzling

sherry vinegar, 2 tbsp

honey, 2 tsp

kosher salt, ½ tsp

freshly ground pepper

pecans, ½ cup (2 oz/60 g) toasted (page 217) and chopped

arugula leaves or other tender greens, 4 cups (4 oz/125 g)

MAKES 4 SERVINGS

Preheat the oven to 350°F (180°C). Cut off the beet tops and reserve for another use. Place the beets in a single layer in a heavy ovenproof frying pan just large enough to accommodate them, and drizzle with olive oil. Cover with aluminum foil. Roast the beets until tender when pierced with a small, sharp knife, about 40 minutes. Let cool slightly, then peel and trim the beets. Cut into rounds about ¼ inch (6 mm) thick.

In a large, shallow serving bowl, whisk together the 2 tbsp olive oil, the vinegar, honey, salt, and a pinch of pepper. Add the beet slices, pecans, and arugula and toss gently. Serve.

roasted root vegetables with winter herbs

extra-virgin olive oil, 3 tbsp

parsnips, ¾ lb (375 g)

carrots, ½ lb (250 g)

russet potatoes, ¾ lb (375 g)

orange-fleshed sweet potatoes, ¾ lb (375 g)

fresh sage leaves, 1 tbsp chopped

fresh thyme leaves, 1 tbsp chopped

fresh rosemary, 1½ tsp chopped

garlic, 3 cloves, minced

kosher salt and freshly ground pepper

MAKES 4–6 SERVINGS

When roasting vegetables, be sure to use a pan large enough to accommodate them in one layer with a little space between them. If the pan is too small, the vegetables will steam instead of getting deliciously browned and caramelized.

Preheat the oven to 425°F (220°C). Brush a large rimmed baking sheet with 1 tbsp of the olive oil. Peel the parsnips and carrots and cut them into 2-inch (5-cm) lengths. Quarter the large ends and halve the smaller ends lengthwise. Halve the potatoes and sweet potatoes and cut them crosswise into slices about ½-inch (12 mm) thick.

In a small bowl, stir together the herbs. In another bowl, combine the vegetables, garlic, the remaining 2 tbsp olive oil, and half of the herb mixture. Toss to mix well. Transfer the vegetables to the prepared baking sheet, spreading them in a single layer. Sprinkle with salt and pepper.

Roast the vegetables, stirring once, until browned and tender, about 40 minutes. Remove from the oven, transfer to a serving dish, sprinkle with the remaining herb mixture, and serve.

Sturdy, colorful winter squashes have harder skins and take longer to mature than their summer squash cousins, and you will need to turn over a large section of your garden to their long, spreading vines. But you will be richly rewarded with their adaptability in the kitchen, where they slip easily into soups and risottos, stews and salads, sautés, and even tacos.

how to grow
winter squashes & pumpkins

plant winter squashes and pumpkins

Growing winter squashes is relatively easy. But you need to allow plenty of space for the vines to spread, as they can sometimes extend 15 feet (5 m). You can purchase nursery starts, but the seeds are big, inexpensive, and sprout easily, which makes them a better choice. Butternut, acorn, and a pumpkin variety are good choices. The soil must be warm enough to give the seedlings a good start, so plant the seeds in late spring or early summer in a spot with full sun. Squashes are traditionally grown on hills—small mounds of soil that allow for good drainage—but raised beds or even a very large container, such as a half wine barrel, will do. If you plan to grow several vines, space the hills about 4 feet (60 cm) apart. Plant the seeds ½ to 1 inch (12 mm to 2.5 cm) deep and about 4 inches (10 cm) apart in rich soil. When the seedlings are 4 inches (10 cm) tall, thin them to about three plants per hill.

maintain winter squashes and pumpkins

Water the plants regularly and deeply, never allowing them to dry out, and keep them adequately fertilized. Train the vines, working gently and moving them a little each day, so they don't go beyond their patch. When the vines are flowering and beginning to form small fruits, check for squash bugs in all stages of life—eggs, nymphs, and mature insects— as this voracious pest will feed on the plants, causing the blossoms and baby squashes to wither and die. Look for clusters of brown eggs on the underside of leaves and crush them between your fingers. Pick off the nymphs, which look like aphids, and kill them in a bucket of soapy water. The mature bugs need to be trapped at night under boards or layers of burlap. Dispose of the trapped bugs as you see fit. My preferred method is feeding them to my chickens.

Acorn squash plants need the most space to spread. They are climbers with lots of heavy fruits and they can easily take over a garden. But pumpkins require the most attention, at least if you want to grow jack-o'-lantern–worthy beauties. Once their vines are established in the "patch," add mulch around the plant bases to keep the roots from drying out and to discourage weeds from growing. When you see blooms and small fruits developing, make sure the vines are well watered. After a few pumpkins have grown to about 6 inches (15 cm) in diameter, pinch off the end of the vine so that the plant's energy goes toward growing big fruits, not more green leaves. Place boards, preferably from recycled wood, under pumpkins to keep them from rotting, and rotate the squashes occasionally to encourage symmetry.

harvest winter squashes and pumpkins

All winter squashes should be harvested before the first frost. They are ready to pick when the skin is hardened to the point that you can no longer puncture it with your fingernail. Be sure not to harvest butternut squashes too early or they will lack flavor. Store squashes for winter use in a cool, dark, dry area. They will keep off the vine for about 1½ months.

orange-glazed acorn squash & cranberries

These fork-tender squash slices, infused with the flavors of citrus and warm spices, are great on the holiday table. But don't file this recipe away to serve only with turkey or ham— it's just too good. I like to serve this dish alongside seared pork chops and braised winter greens, which makes my family thankful that we eat just as well any time of year.

Preheat the oven to 400°F (200°C). Butter a large rimmed baking sheet or a 9-by-13-by-2-inch (23-by-33-by-5-cm) baking dish.

In a saucepan over medium-high heat, combine the butter, orange juice and zest, coriander seeds, and allspice, bring to a boil, and boil until reduced to ¾ cup (6 fl oz/180 ml), 3—4 minutes. Remove from the heat.

Trim the ends from the squash, cut in half lengthwise, then cut each half lengthwise into slices about 1 inch (2.5 cm) thick. Arrange the squash slices on the prepared baking sheet, and drizzle the orange juice mixture over the top. Sprinkle with salt and pepper and toss gently to coat.

Bake the squash slices until just tender when pierced with a small, sharp knife, about 20 minutes. Add the cranberries, gently turn the squash slices, and bake until the slices are lightly glazed, about 4 minutes longer. Transfer the squash and cranberries to a platter and serve.

unsalted butter, ¼ cup (2 oz/ 60 g), plus more for baking dish

fresh orange juice, 1¼ cups (10 fl oz/310 ml)

orange zest, 1 tsp grated

coriander seeds, 1 tsp coarsely crushed in a mortar

ground allspice, ½ tsp

acorn squash, 2

kosher salt and freshly ground pepper

dried cranberries, ¼ cup (1½ oz/45 g)

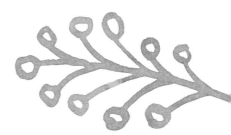

roasted acorn squash salad with candied pecans, pears & curry vinaigrette

MAKES 2–4 SERVINGS

olive oil, 4 tbsp (2 fl oz/60 ml), plus more for baking sheet

acorn squash, 1, halved, seeded, peeled, and cut into ¾-inch (2-cm) cubes

curry powder, 1½ tsp

kosher salt and freshly ground pepper

shallot, 2 tbsp minced

white balsamic vinegar, 2 tbsp

garlic, 1 clove, pressed

salad greens, 6 cups (6 oz/185 g)

pear, 1 large, peeled, cored, and diced

fresh goat cheese, 2 oz (60 g), crumbled

candied pecans (page 216), ½ cup (2 oz/60 g)

Juicy pears and richly flavored acorn squash prove that salad isn't just for summer. I love this blend of spice, vegetable, fruit and crunch—it can really cheer you up on a cloudy, wintry day. You may need to try a few different brands of curry powder before you find one you like. A medium-hot Madras-style powder would complement this salad.

Preheat the oven to 400°F (200°C). Brush a large, heavy rimmed baking sheet with oil. Place the squash in a bowl, drizzle with 1 tbsp of the oil, sprinkle with 1 tsp of the curry powder, and toss to coat evenly. Spread the squash cubes evenly on the prepared baking sheet, and sprinkle with salt and pepper.

Roast the squash cubes, stirring once, until tender and golden brown, 23–25 minutes. Let cool completely.

To make the vinaigrette, in a small bowl, whisk together the shallot, vinegar, garlic, the remaining ½ tsp curry powder, and the remaining 3 tbsp oil.

In a large bowl, combine the salad greens, squash, and pear. Add about two-thirds of the vinaigrette and toss to coat. Taste and add more vinaigrette if needed. Sprinkle the salad with the goat cheese and pecans and serve.

In a large, heavy pot over medium heat, melt the butter. Add the onion and sauté until tender, about 8 minutes. Stir in the garlic and sage and sauté for 1 minute. Add the squash, apples, and 5 cups (40 fl oz/1.25 l) broth, cover, and simmer until the squash is very tender, about 20 minutes.

Remove from the heat and let cool slightly. Using an immersion blender or standing blender, purée the soup until smooth. If using a standing blender, work in batches, if necessary. (The soup can be cooled, covered, and refrigerated for up to 3 days.)

Return the soup to the pot and warm it over medium heat until the soup reaches a simmer, thinning with additional broth if necessary. Season with salt and pepper. Ladle into bowls and serve.

In a food processor, combine the squash and garlic and pulse until the squash is chopped into ½-inch (12-mm) pieces.

In a large, heavy saucepan over high heat, warm the olive oil. Add the onion and sauté until golden brown and tender, about 4 minutes. Add the squash mixture and ¼ tsp salt and sauté until the squash is almost tender, about 5 minutes. Add the rice and stir for 1 minute. Stir in the wine, broth, rosemary, sage, and 1 tsp of the thyme and bring to a simmer. Reduce the heat to medium-low and simmer, stirring frequently, until the rice is tender and the risotto is thick and creamy, about 30 minutes.

Stir in the Parmesan and season with salt and pepper. Spoon into warmed shallow bowls and sprinkle with the remaining 1 tsp thyme, dividing it evenly. Serve.

butternut-apple soup with sage

unsalted butter, 2 tbsp

yellow onion, 1, sliced

garlic, 2 cloves

fresh sage leaves, 1 tbsp chopped

butternut squash, 4 lb (2 kg), halved, seeded, peeled, and cut into chunks

apples, 2, peeled, halved, cored, and cut into chunks

chicken broth, 5–6 cups (1.25–1.5 l)

kosher salt and freshly ground pepper

butternut squash risotto

butternut squash, 2 cups (8 oz/250 g) peeled and cubed

garlic, 2 cloves

extra-virgin olive oil, 3 tbsp

yellow onion, 1, chopped

kosher salt and freshly ground pepper

Arborio rice, 1½ cups (10½ oz/330 g)

white wine, ¼ cup (2 fl oz/60 ml)

chicken broth, 5½ cups (1.4 l)

fresh rosemary, 1 tsp chopped

fresh sage leaves, 1 tsp chopped

fresh thyme leaves, 2 tsp

Parmesan cheese, ½ cup (2 oz/60 g) grated

crispy pumpkin tacos with pumpkin seed— poblano pesto

poblano chiles, 2 large

for the pesto

fresh cilantro leaves, 1 cup (1 oz/30 g) packed

hulled raw pumpkin seeds, 1 cup (5 oz/155 g)

garlic, 1 clove

olive oil, 2 tbsp

kosher salt

for the filling

olive oil, 1 tbsp

yellow onion, 1 small, chopped

garlic, 4 cloves, minced

ground cumin, 1 tbsp

ancho chile powder or chili powder, 1 tbsp

dried oregano, 2 tsp

pumpkin, 1½ cups (9 oz/280 g) peeled and cut into ¾-inch (2-cm) cubes

feta cheese, ¼ lb (125 g), crumbled

corn oil for griddle

corn tortillas, 16, each 6 inches (15 cm) in diameter

Monterey jack cheese, 1 lb (500 g), shredded

Mexican hot-pepper sauce such as Valentina

MAKES 6–8 SERVINGS

You can serve these pumpkin tacos as an *antojito* (appetizer) at a party, or as the centerpiece of a casual dinner, but mostly you'll want to eat them standing in the kitchen, hot off the griddle, and doused with hot sauce—they're that irresistible.

Using tongs, hold 1 poblano chile over the flame of a gas burner, turning it as needed, until charred and blistered on all sides. Repeat with the second chile. Alternatively, preheat the broiler, place the poblano chiles on a baking sheet, and broil, turning, until blackened on all sides. Place the chiles in a bowl. Cover the bowl with plastic wrap and leave until cool. Peel off the blackened skin, remove the stems and seeds, then chop.

To make the pesto, in a food processor, combine half of the poblano chiles, the cilantro, pumpkin seeds, and garlic and pulse until finely chopped. Add the olive oil and process until almost smooth. Add about 4 tbsp (2 fl oz/60 ml) water, 1 tbsp at a time, and process until well blended and the mixture is thick but spreadable. You may not need all of the water. Season with salt.

To make the filling, in a large, heavy frying pan over medium heat, warm the olive oil. Add the onion and garlic and sauté until almost tender, about 4 minutes. Sprinkle in the cumin, ancho chile powder, and oregano and sauté for 1 minute longer. Add the pumpkin and ¼ cup (2 fl oz/60 ml) water, cover, and cook until the pumpkin is tender, about 10 minutes. Uncover and cook until the water evaporates, about 2 minutes. Remove from the heat and coarsely mash the pumpkin with a fork or potato masher. Gently mix in the remaining poblano chile and the feta cheese.

Preheat a large griddle or frying pan over medium-high heat. Brush the griddle or pan with corn oil. While the griddle is heating up, fill the tacos. Spread 2 tbsp pumpkin filling over half of 1 corn tortilla. Top the filling with 1 generous tbsp pesto, some of the jack cheese, and a few drops of hot-pepper sauce. Fold the uncovered half of the tortilla over the filling to close. Repeat until all the tacos are filled.

Working in batches, fry the tacos, turning once, until crisp on both sides and the cheese has melted, about 3 minutes per side, brushing the griddle with more oil as needed to prevent scorching. Serve.

Rosemary, sage, and thyme are hearty perennials that can be planted in a vegetable or herb plot, make a fragrant ornamental addition to a flower bed, and even flourish in pots. In the kitchen, I use them to flavor a homey onion soup, in a spread for grilled ham and cheese sandwiches that appeal to children and grown-ups alike, or to give a savory bread pudding an herbal accent.

how to grow winter herbs

plant and maintain rosemary, sage, and thyme in pots
Purchase nursery starts or use cuttings for the best results. In cold-weather zones, plant the herbs in pots in rich, well-draining soil. Make sure the containers are large enough to accommodate the root structures of the plants, and water the plants carefully and consistently, allowing the soil to become "just dry" between applications. Rosemary, sage, and thyme all need several hours of direct sunshine every day, so if you plan to "winter" your potted herbs indoors, situate them where they will get plenty of sunlight, or consider using a grow light on winter's darkest days.

plant and maintain rosemary, sage, and thyme in the garden
Growing rosemary, sage, and thyme directly in the ground is simple: use starts or cuttings and space them about 2 feet (60 cm) apart for rosemary and sage, and about 1 foot (30 cm) apart for thyme. Like their potted cousins, they need full sun and well-draining soil. Of the three, sage is the most finicky because it tends to be hypersensitive to water. Situate sage plants in an area clear of irrigation and water infrequently, verging on the neglectful. Thyme prefers dry conditions, too, though it is not as fussy as sage. Rosemary grows like groundcover on the surrounding hills of my neighborhood, but it doesn't tolerate cold weather.

harvest rosemary, sage, and thyme
Clip sprigs and leaves as needed. All three herbs can get leggy and woody if they are not trimmed back after they flower. In warmer areas, the trio will do as well in summer as they do in winter. In colder climates, prune the herbs in the fall and surround the plants with mulch. Sage and thyme are wonderful dried, so if you live in a cold climate and cannot winter your plants indoors, harvest them in the fall and dry them (see page 114).

grilled ham & cheese sandwiches with winter herb pistou

for the pistou

fresh sage leaves, 1½ tbsp chopped

fresh thyme leaves, 1½ tbsp chopped

fresh rosemary, 1½ tsp chopped

fresh flat-leaf Italian parsley, 1 tbsp chopped

garlic, 1 clove, chopped

kosher salt, ¼ tsp

walnut oil, 2 tbsp

French or sourdough bread, 8 slices

Gruyère or white Cheddar cheese, 6 oz (185 g), thinly sliced

Black Forest ham, 3 oz (90 g), thinly sliced

unsalted butter, for cooking

Pistou is pesto with a French accent. Here, it takes the common grilled ham and cheese sandwich to dinner-worthy level. I also love drizzling the pistou on fried eggs. I often use a panini grill, but a frying pan or griddle will do just fine.

To make the pistou, in a mortar, combine the sage, thyme, rosemary, parsley, garlic, salt, and walnut oil. Grind together with a pestle until the herbs and garlic are crushed and all the ingredients are well blended.

Preheat a panini grill or a griddle to medium-high, or preheat a large frying pan over medium-high heat. Meanwhile, spread 4 slices of the bread with the pistou, dividing it evenly. Top the pistou with half of the cheese and all of the ham, dividing it evenly. Top the ham with the remaining cheese, dividing it evenly. Top the sandwiches with the remaining bread slices.

Butter the hot grill, griddle, or pan. Add the sandwiches and cook until they are golden brown on both sides and the cheese has melted, about 8 minutes. Cut each sandwich in half and serve.

savory bread pudding with sage & aged gouda

coarse country bread, ½ lb (250 g)

extra-virgin olive oil, 2 tbsp

garlic, 2 cloves, pressed

unsalted butter, 1 tbsp, plus more
for baking dish

shallot, 1 large, finely chopped

fresh sage leaves, 2 tbsp chopped

large eggs, 4

heavy cream, 1¾ cups
(14 fl oz/430 ml)

whole milk, 1 cup (8 fl oz/250 ml)

kosher salt, ½ tsp

freshly ground pepper, ½ tsp

aged Gouda cheese, 1½ cups
(6 oz/185 g) grated

MAKES 6 SERVINGS

This is wonderful for breakfast or brunch, especially when paired with sausages or ham. It's ideal for entertaining in the morning because it can be assembled the night before baking, and you won't have to wake as early as a farmer to produce this warm, rich, and cheesy dish.

Preheat the oven to 375°F (190°C). Cut the bottom crust and short ends off the bread and discard. Cut the remaining bread into 1-inch (2.5-cm) cubes. You should have about 5 cups (10 oz/315 g) loosely packed. In the bottom of a large bowl, stir together the olive oil and garlic. Add the bread cubes and toss to coat evenly. Transfer the bread to a large rimmed baking sheet, spreading it in an even layer.

Bake the cubes, stirring occasionally, until golden and lightly crunchy, about 20 minutes. Remove from the oven.

Meanwhile, in a heavy frying pan over medium heat, melt the 1 tbsp butter. Add the shallot and sauté until translucent, about 4 minutes. Add the sage and stir until it turns dark green and fragrant, about 2 minutes. Remove from the heat and let cool.

Generously butter an 8-inch (20-cm) square baking dish. In a large bowl, whisk together the eggs, cream, milk, salt, and pepper. Stir in the shallot-sage mixture and 1 cup (4 oz/125 g) of the cheese. Add the bread cubes and stir to coat. Transfer the mixture to the prepared dish and let stand for 20 minutes. (The dish can be loosely covered with plastic wrap and refrigerated for up to 1 day before continuing.)

Sprinkle the top with the remaining ½ cup (2 oz/60 g) cheese. Bake until the bread pudding is set and the top is golden, about 45 minutes. Serve warm or at room temperature.

roast chicken with herb & spice rub

The combination of herbs and spices on this bird create a flavorful coating that will make you want to savor every last bit. Cutting the chicken in half before roasting ensures that it roasts evenly and quickly and the skin gets nice and crisp.

Preheat the oven to 400°F (200°C). Grate ½ tsp zest from the lemon into a small bowl. Add the garlic, sage, thyme, rosemary, coriander, paprika, and allspice and stir to blend.

Place the chicken, cut side up, on a large, heavy rimmed baking sheet. Brush the cut side of the chicken with olive oil. Rub half of the herb mixture over the oiled surface and sprinkle with salt and pepper. Turn the chicken over and brush the skin side with olive oil. Rub the oiled surface with the remaining herb mixture and sprinkle with salt and pepper.

Roast the chicken until golden brown and an instant-read thermometer inserted into the thickest part of a thigh registers 160°F (70°C), about 40 minutes. Transfer the chicken to a platter.

Place the baking sheet on the stove top over medium heat and add the wine. Bring to a boil and deglaze, stirring to scrape up any browned bits on the baking sheet. Add the broth and boil until the liquid is reduced to about 1 cup (8 fl oz/250 ml), about 3 minutes. Remove from the heat. Cut the lemon in half and squeeze half into the sauce. Season with salt, pepper, and lemon juice to taste, then pour into a warmed serving bowl. Cut the chicken into pieces and serve, passing the sauce at the table.

lemon, 1

garlic, 2 cloves, minced

fresh sage leaves, 1 tbsp minced

fresh thyme leaves, 1 tbsp minced

fresh rosemary, 1 tsp minced

ground coriander, 1 tsp

paprika, ½ tsp

ground allspice, ¼ tsp

chicken, 1 whole, about 4 lb (2 kg), cut in half through the breastbone

extra-virgin olive oil, for brushing

kosher salt and freshly ground pepper

dry white wine, ½ cup

chicken broth, 1 cup (8 fl oz/250 ml)

This adaptation of French onion soup boasts bacon and a generous measure of herbs, in addition to the classic cheese-topped toasts. I particularly like it on a cold day, especially with a glass of full-bodied Belgian ale or a homebrew.

In a large, heavy pot over medium heat, fry the bacon until the fat is rendered and the bacon is crisp, about 4 minutes. Using a slotted spoon, transfer the bacon to a small bowl.

Add the onions to the drippings in the pot, reduce the heat to medium-low, and cook, stirring occasionally, until very tender, about 30 minutes. Add the garlic and continue cooking until the onions are golden brown and very soft, about 20 minutes longer. Pour in the wine and cook until the wine evaporates and the onions are brown and jamlike, about 12 minutes. Add the broth, bay leaf, and rosemary, sage, and thyme sprigs and simmer the soup very gently to meld the flavors, about 20 minutes. Remove and discard the herb sprigs. (The soup can be cooled, covered, and refrigerated for up to 3 days. Reheat to serving temperature before continuing.)

Preheat the broiler. Arrange the toasts on a small rimmed baking sheet and sprinkle evenly with the cheese. Broil the toasts just until the cheese melts. Remove from the broiler, sprinkle with the bacon and minced herbs, and return to the broiler. Broil until the toasts are heated through.

Ladle the soup into warmed bowls. Top with the toasts, dividing them evenly, and serve.

onion soup with bacon, winter herbs & gruyere

applewood-smoked bacon, 6 oz (185 g), cut into ¼-inch (6-mm) pieces

yellow onions, 3 large, thinly sliced

garlic, 4 cloves, chopped

dry white wine, ⅓ cup (3 fl oz/80 ml)

beef broth, 8 cups (2 l)

bay leaf, 1

fresh rosemary, 1 large sprig, plus ½ tsp minced

fresh sage, 1 large sprig, plus ½ tsp minced

fresh thyme, 1 large sprig, plus ½ tsp minced

baguette, 18 thin slices, toasted

Gruyère cheese, ¾ cup (3 oz/90 g) shredded

With apples and pears from the cooler climes, and citrus from warmer areas, it's easy to enjoy fruit throughout the fall and winter. Crisp apples are my grab-and-go snack, and juicy pears are a relished event. Apples and pears scent the entire house when spiced and cooked into treats. When the days grow shorter and colder, citrus—such as the lemons, blood oranges, and limes plucked from my backyard trees— provide a burst of sunshine in colorful salads and tangy desserts.

how to grow citrus, apples & pears

plant and maintain citrus

Don't plant citrus trees unless you can provide them with large doses of both sunshine and heat. Grapefruits, oranges, limes, lemons, kumquats, and tangerines are all relatively easy to grow. Again, consult your local nursery for which varieties do best in your area. I have a Bearss lime tree that yields fruit practically year-round, with a bumper crop in February. My Moro orange doesn't require quite as much heat as other oranges, such as navel or Valencia, and the tree holds an attractive shape with little or no pruning.

The Eureka lemon, the variety most commonly in markets, is a good choice because the fruit is uniform, juicy, and tart. The tree is not thorny like some lemon varieties, and it produces fruit in late fall and again in early spring. The round, thin-skinned Meyer lemon is less acidic and more aromatic than the Eureka. The tree is less fussy than other lemon trees and is also smaller, making it a good fit for a small yard. In colder areas, consider growing it in a pot and allowing it to summer outdoors and winter in a greenhouse.

Plant citrus trees in well-draining soil in a sunny spot, preferably near a wall that can provide protection if an unexpected freeze occurs. Dig a hole about 3 feet (1 m) in diameter and as deep as the plastic pot the tree comes in. When filling the hole with good potting soil, be careful not to cover the tree's root crown. Keep the trees well watered.

plant and maintain apples and pears

Growing apples and pears requires cool to temperate weather, space, and plenty of care. Consult the experts at your local nursery for which varieties grow well in your area and which will pollinate one another. Once you have chosen your trees, plant at least two trees that bloom at the same time within at least 30 feet (10 m) of each other to ensure pollination.

Plan on putting the trees in the ground in early spring when the plants are dormant. Dig a hole about 2 feet (60 cm) wide and 2 feet (60 cm) deep to accommodate the roots. Water well, but don't overfertilize, which can cause blight. Pick the fruits when just underripe in fall and store them for use throughout the winter months. At the end of winter, consult the experts once again on the best way to prune.

radicchio, orange & hazelnut salad

oranges, 3

hazelnuts, ¼ cup (1¼ oz/40 g) toasted and skins removed (page 217)

hazelnut oil, 3 tbsp

sherry vinegar, 1 tbsp

honey, 1 tsp

kosher salt and freshly ground pepper

radicchio, 1 head, separated into leaves and torn

shallot, 1, thinly sliced

MAKES 4 SERVINGS

The colors of this salad are dramatic: deep burgundy leaves, orange citrus, white shallot slices, and toasty brown nuts. You can use any variety of orange—navels, blood oranges, or rosy Cara Caras are all equally delicious. I serve this alongside Butternut-Apple Soup with Sage or Butternut Squash Risotto (both on page 157).

Using a sharp serrated knife, cut a thin slice off the top and bottom of 1 orange to expose the flesh. Stand the orange upright and cut off the peel and pith, slicing downward and following the contour of the fruit. Cut the orange crosswise into rounds. Repeat with the remaining 2 oranges.

Roughly chop the hazelnuts. In a serving bowl, whisk together the hazelnut oil, vinegar, and honey. Season with salt and pepper.

Add the radicchio leaves, shallot, and orange slices to the serving bowl and toss to coat evenly with the vinaigrette. Sprinkle with the toasted hazelnuts and serve.

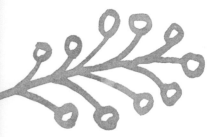

Lemon curd is lovely spread on butter biscuits for an afternoon snack. Or, try mixing it with sour cream—four parts lemon curd to one part sour cream—spoon the mixture into prebaked tartlet shells (page 215), and top each tartlet with a dollop of whipped cream.

In a heavy saucepan, whisk together the sugar, whole eggs, and egg yolks until well blended. Whisk in the lemon juice and zest. Place over medium heat and cook, whisking constantly, until the curd thickens and comes to a boil, about 3 minutes. Remove from the heat and whisk in the butter.

Let cool, then use right away, or store in an airtight container in the refrigerator for up to 2 weeks.

tangy lemon curd

sugar, ½ cup (4 oz/125 g)

large whole eggs, 2

large egg yolks, 2

fresh lemon juice, ⅓ cup (3 fl oz/80 ml)

lemon zest, 2 tsp grated

unsalted butter, 1 tbsp

In a medium saucepan over medium heat, combine 2 cups (16 fl oz/ 500 ml) water, the sugar, and the lemon zest and heat, stirring, until the sugar dissolves and the syrup comes to a boil. Remove from the heat and let cool completely.

Stir the lemon juice into the cooled syrup, then pour the mixture into an 8-inch (20-cm) square baking dish. Freeze the mixture, whisking it every 45 minutes to break up the ice crystals, until it is frozen solid, about 4 hours total. (It will keep in the freezer for up to 4 days.)

Just before serving, pour the cream into a chilled metal bowl. Using the tip of a sharp knife, scrape the seeds from the vanilla bean into the bowl. Using a whisk or a handheld mixer, whip the cream until soft peaks form. Whisk in the limoncello and continue whisking until soft peaks form again.

Using a fork, repeatedly scrape the surface of the granita to form light crystals. Spoon the granita into chilled glasses, and top each serving with a spoonful of cream. Serve.

meyer lemon granita with limoncello & vanilla cream

sugar, 1 cup (8 oz/250 g)

Meyer lemon zest, 1 tsp grated

fresh Meyer lemon juice, ⅔ cup (5 fl oz/160 ml)

heavy cream, ¾ cup (6 fl oz/180 ml) cold

vanilla bean, 2-inch (5-cm) piece, split lengthwise

limoncello, 3 tbsp

glazed lime-almond pound cake

for the cake

slivered almonds, 1 cup
(4½ oz/140 g)

confectioners' sugar, 1 cup
(4 oz/125 g)

large eggs, 3 whole, plus
1 separated

unbleached all-purpose flour,
2 cups (10 oz/315 g)

baking powder, 1 tsp

kosher salt, ¾ tsp

granulated sugar, 1 cup
(8 oz/250 g)

lime zest, 1 tsp grated

unsalted butter, 1 cup (8 oz/
250 g), at room temperature

fresh lime juice, 3 tbsp

whole milk, ¼ cup (2 fl oz/60 ml)

for the glaze

confectioners' sugar, 1 cup
(4 oz/125 g) plus 2 tbsp

lime zest, ½ tsp grated

fresh lime juice, about 4½ tsp

MAKES 1 LOAF CAKE

Lime adds a lovely perfume to the delicate almond flavor in this moist pound cake. This is the kind of cake that draws you to it, enjoying slices and slivers of it until only a crumb remains. Best to serve it to friends with a fragrant Earl Grey tea, or dress up the slices with whipped cream, Tangy Lemon Curd (page 173), and orange slices for a sunny winter dessert.

Preheat the oven to 325°F (165°C). Line the bottom and sides of a 9-by-5-by-3-inch (23-by-13-by-7.5-cm) loaf pan with parchment paper.

In a food processor, combine the almonds and confectioners' sugar and process until the almonds are finely ground. Add the egg white (reserve the yolk) and process until a thick paste forms. Set aside.

In a large bowl, whisk together the flour, baking powder, and salt. In another bowl, using a handheld mixer on medium speed, beat together the granulated sugar and lime zest to release the essential oils in the zest. Add the butter and beat until light and fluffy. Gradually add the reserved almond paste and beat until well mixed. Add the whole eggs and the egg yolk, one at a time, beating well after each addition. On low speed, mix in half of the flour mixture and then the lime juice. Mix in the remaining flour mixture, followed by the milk, mixing just until thoroughly combined.

Pour the batter into the prepared pan and smooth the top. Bake until a toothpick inserted into the center of the cake comes out clean, about 1 hour and 10 minutes. Let cool in the pan on a wire rack for 10 minutes. Run a small, sharp knife around the inside edge of the pan to loosen the cake sides, then turn the cake out onto the rack and let cool completely.

To make the glaze, in a bowl, whisk together the confectioners' sugar, lime zest, and 4 tsp of the lime juice until well blended and smooth. Add an additional ½ tsp lime juice if necessary to thin to drizzling consistency.

Place the cake on a serving plate and drizzle the glaze over the top, letting it run down the sides. Let stand until the glaze sets. Serve, or cover with plastic wrap and store at cool room temperature for up to 1 day.

caramel-sautéed apples

The key to making these caramel-coated apples is to avoid stirring them with a spoon, as the caramel will stick to it. Instead, toss the apples around in the pan by deftly moving the pan back and forth over the burner. The apples are lovely on their own or with ice cream. Or they make a great rustic tart filling (see Savory Pastry Dough, page 215).

In a large, heavy frying pan over medium-high heat, melt the butter. Add the sugar and cook, without stirring, until the sugar melts and turns nut brown, about 2 minutes. Immediately add the apple slices to the pan and reduce the heat to medium. Cook the apples, shifting the pan back and forth over the burner to redistribute the apples occasionally, until they are tender and browned, about 15 minutes.

Pour the cream over the apples and then swirl the pan so that any caramel on the sides dissolves into the cream. Continue cooking until the caramel darkens slightly and the apples are nicely coated, about 1 minute. Transfer to a serving bowl and serve.

unsalted butter, 1 tbsp

sugar, ⅓ cup (3 oz/90 g)

apples, 3, peeled, halved, cored, and sliced

heavy cream, ¼ cup (2 fl oz/60 ml)

In a large, heavy saucepan, combine the sherry, ½ cup (4 fl oz/125 ml) water, the brown sugar, and the honey. Using the tip of a sharp knife, scrape the seeds from the vanilla bean into the pan. Place over medium heat and bring to a simmer. Cover and simmer gently for about 5 minutes.

Add the pears, cover, reduce the heat to low, and simmer until tender when pierced with a small, sharp knife, about 10 minutes. Using a slotted spoon, transfer the pears to a bowl.

Raise the heat to high, bring the syrup to a boil, and boil until reduced to a thin glaze, about 4 minutes. Pour the glaze over the pears.

Serve the pears warm or cold with the ice cream and chocolate sauce.

vanilla-poached pears with bittersweet chocolate—honey sauce

sherry, ½ cup (4 fl oz/125 ml)

golden brown sugar, 2 tbsp firmly packed

honey, 2 tbsp

vanilla bean, 1, split lengthwise

Bosc pears, 3 large, peeled, quartered, and cored

vanilla ice cream, for serving

bittersweet chocolate—honey sauce (page 213)

MAKES ABOUT 1½ CUPS (15 OZ/470 G)

Roasted pear butter is great on toast and scones, but I like it best spread thickly on whole-grain bread with almond butter. This memorable twist on PB&J is great when you're on the go.

Position a rack in the lower third of the oven and preheat to 400°F (200°C). Butter a large rimmed baking sheet. Peel, quarter, and core the pears, then cut each quarter in half crosswise. In a bowl, combine the pears and butter and toss to coat evenly. Spread the pears in a single layer on the prepared baking sheet. Sprinkle the brown sugar evenly over the pears.

Roast the pears until tender when pierced with a small, sharp knife and browned on the edges, about 30 minutes. Remove from the oven and transfer the pears and all the caramelized juices on the bottom of the pan to a food processor. Let stand until cool.

Process the cooled pears until smooth. Add the honey and process to combine. Transfer the pear butter to a clean jar, cap tightly, and refrigerate for up to 2 weeks.

roasted pear butter

unsalted butter, 2 tbsp, melted, plus more for the baking sheet

Bosc or Comice pears, 5 small, about 1½ lb (700 g) total weight

golden brown sugar, 2 tbsp firmly packed

honey, 2 tbsp

brandied apple cake with figs & walnuts

dried Mission figs, ¾ cup diced (about 4½ oz/ 140 g)

brandy, ¼ cup (2 fl oz/60 ml)

unsalted butter, ¾ cup (6 oz/ 185 g), plus more for the pan

unbleached all-purpose flour, 1½ cups (7½ oz/235 g)

baking soda, 1 tsp

ground cinnamon, 2 tsp

ground cardamom, 1 tsp

ground cloves, ½ tsp

kosher salt, ¾ tsp

granulated sugar, ⅔ cup (5 oz/155 g)

golden brown sugar, ⅔ cup firmly packed (5 oz/155 g)

large eggs, 2

tart apples, 4 cups (1 lb/500 g) peeled and chopped

walnuts, 1 cup (4 oz/125 g), toasted (page 217) and chopped

Loaded with apple chunks, dried fruit, and nuts, here is a not-overly-sweet cake that can be enjoyed for breakfast, afternoon tea, or as a casual dessert when topped with whipped cream. Beautiful in its simplicity—I bake and serve it straight from a baking pan that belonged to my grandmother—this moist cake will disappear as quickly as you can make it.

In a small bowl, combine the figs and brandy and let stand while you prepare the remaining ingredients.

Preheat the oven to 350°F (180°C). Generously butter a 9-inch (23-cm) square pan.

In a bowl, whisk together the flour, baking soda, cinnamon, cardamom, cloves, and salt. In a large bowl, using a handheld mixer on medium speed, beat together the butter, granulated sugar, and brown sugar until light and fluffy. Add the eggs, one at a time, beating well after each addition. Mix in the flour mixture on low speed. Add the apples, walnuts, and fig-brandy mixture and stir just until combined.

Pour the batter into the prepared pan and smooth the top. Bake until a toothpick inserted into the center of the cake comes out clean, about 1 hour. Let cool completely in the pan on a wire rack.

Cut into squares to serve, or cover tightly with plastic wrap and store at room temperature for up to 3 days.

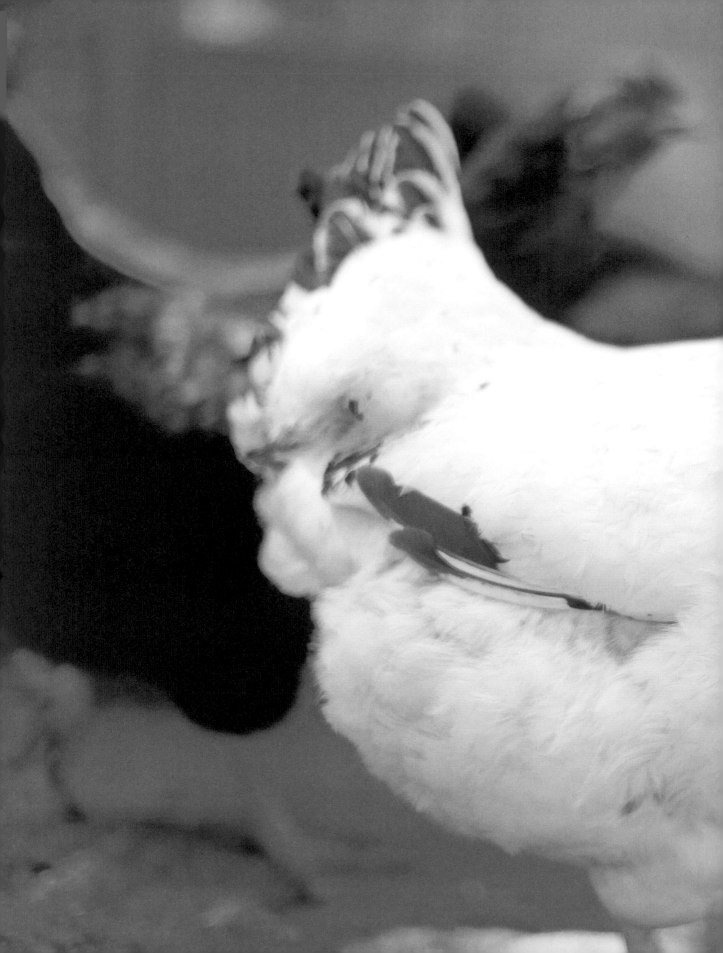

THE COOP
& THE HIVE

AN INTRODUCTION TO CHICKENS

The rewards of keeping chickens in the backyard are many. First, chickens make great pets: they are easy to care for, charming to observe, and don't require much space. If you garden, you can't beat chicken manure as fertilizer. But the best thing about keeping hens, hands down, is the eggs. What other pet provides you with something as wholesome and delicious as a freshly laid egg? Plus, eggs are wonderfully versatile, used for frittatas and scrambles, quiches and custards, sauces and salads.

choosing your chickens

Raising baby chicks is easy and a lot of fun, especially when kids are involved. A trip to the feed store or hatchery or a box in the mail (yes, a box in the mail!) delivers soft, fluffy peepers. If you are buying in person, choose lively, loud chicks with clean bottoms. If you are using a mail-order source, try to buy the chicks from a nearby hatchery so that they won't need to travel too far.

Choose breeds that are good layers and well suited to your climate. If it snows where you live, find birds that can withstand cold winters. I live where the summer is very hot, so I want chickens that can take the heat. My favorite breeds are Plymouth Rock, Australorp, Buff Orpington, Red Sex-Link, Black Sex-Link, and the Araucana hens that lay pale blue eggs. Buy chicks when the weather is relatively warm, so that once they are moved outside, they don't shiver in the cold.

When deciding how many chicks to purchase, you'll need figure out how big a flock you would like, then factor in the chances of one of them growing into a rooster or not surviving. Chickens are social animals and should be raised in groups of two or more. Four good laying hens will provide about a dozen and a half eggs per week in the spring and summer, so I would recommend starting with five or six chicks.

raising baby chicks

In the beginning, all you'll need to care for chicks are a cardboard box, newspapers, a small waterer, a light fixture or heating pad, and food. I line a wine case–size cardboard box with several layers of newspaper and place a waterer in one corner and a feeder in another corner. The waterer is a small dish that screws onto a water-filled jar that releases water into the dish when the jar is inverted. The feeder is a covered dish with openings that allow the chicks to eat the feed in the dish without scratching, roosting, or pooping in their food. The feeder, waterer, and starter feed are all available at a feed store. (If your chicks have not been vaccinated against coccidiosis, an intestinal disease, be sure to buy medicated starter feed.) I usually buy 20 lb (10 kg) of starter feed when the chicks arrive and switch to regular laying mash or pellets when I run out. Change and refresh the feed and water often, and keep the box clean by replacing soiled newspapers.

Chicks need to be kept warm, clean, and dry. Baby chicks should be kept at 90°F (32°C) for the first week, then 5°F (3°C) cooler each subsequent week. To keep chicks warm, clip a work light fitted with a 60-watt bulb to the side of the box, or put an electric heating pad under the box. A thermometer isn't necessary. You'll be able to tell if your chicks are too hot or too cold by observing them: if they are huddled tightly, they are cold; if they are keeping their distance from one another and seem listless, they are too hot. Chicks like to sleep in a pile, but they should look like a soft mound of feathers, not a tight cluster.

After a week or two, you might only need to use the lightbulb or heating pad at night. Your chicks will grow quickly and will need to be transferred to a larger box when they become crowded. As your chicks begin to test their feathers, you will want to cover the box with a screen to keep them confined.

USING CHICKEN MANURE

Chicken manure is an excellent fertilizer. It's high in nitrogen, phosphorus, and potassium. Like all manure, it cannot be added directly to the soil in your vegetable garden and flower beds because the fresh nutrients can burn the plants' root structures. To age chicken manure, rake it into a pile with other garden scraps such as grass clippings or leaves and let it stand for two to three months. At my house, we rake the chicken yard weekly and add the manure to our existing compost pile, where it is combined with other green waste and allowed to age with an occasional mixing. Although everyone in my family likes to think that our green thumbs are responsible for our amazing vegetable haul each season, we realize that much of the credit goes to the chickens for providing us with such rich fertilizer.

chicken coops and the great outdoors

At about four weeks, the chicks "feather out" (grow feathers all over), and you can begin to keep them outdoors. That means you will need a place to put them. Technically, you don't need a coop to raise hens; they just need a place to stay dry, a shelter from the wind, shade from the sun, and protection from predators, such as raccoons, dogs, and other animals. A coop can be an old doghouse, playhouse, or a custom structure.

Situate the coop where there is shade, so your chickens can stay cool in the summer. You also want it to have exposure to the sun, however, as chickens like to be warm when the weather cools. Make sure that the site has good drainage, too, to prevent water from collecting around the coop during the rainy season. A coop can be any size, but plan on about 3 square feet (0.25 sq m) of yard space per chicken. Our coop is a 7-by-4-foot (2.1-by-1.2-m) shedlike structure with a 5-foot (1.5-m) ceiling, a secure door, and wire-covered openings for air. There is a 3-by-1½-foot (1-by-0.5-meter) nesting box with a hatch opening to the outside for egg collection. It sits in a oak-shaded, chicken wire–enclosed yard. Chickens sleep or roost at night on perches, which can be poles or tree branches.

feeding your flock

Chickens will survive on vegetable scraps and bugs foraged in the yard, but for the best egg production, feed your hens commercial laying mash or pellets formulated with high amounts of protein. The feed also supplies the hens with calcium for strong eggshells and with the grit—sand and small pebbles—needed to digest food properly.

My family and I enjoy causing a minor feeding frenzy in the chicken yard by arriving with our chickens' favorite foods, such as oxalis weeds or melon seeds and rinds. Chickens peck and scratch the ground all day long, so give them something colorful to tear at. I give my chickens all sorts of kitchen scraps, such as carrot and potato peels, apple and pear cores, stems from herbs, and corncobs. The variety seems to make them very happy, and I'm sure their eggs taste richer due to their colorful diet.

Although you could just let your chickens fend for themselves and forage for food in your garden, I have learned that giving chickens complete freedom to roam your yard has its drawbacks. Chickens like the same foods that we do and will wreak havoc on your heirloom tomatoes, baby lettuces, and precious berries. They also will lay fewer eggs, and when they do lay, it will often be in hard-to-find places. Domestication has its pluses.

Make sure that your chickens always have access to clean water, especially in the summer. An automatic waterer attached to a hose valve is particularly handy, as the water stays fresh and is replenished as the hens drink.

eggs, glorious eggs

Hens start laying eggs at five months. At first, you might find peewee eggs, but as your hens get older, their eggs get larger. Egg production is best in summer when days are long and sunny. With winter's shorter days, fewer eggs will be laid, and the number could dwindle to as few as one a week.

Encourage your hens to lay their eggs in a nesting box or other convenient place for gathering them. A nesting box should be a bit bigger than a chicken and a few inches off the ground. It can be made from nearly any material—wood, plastic, metal—but should be easy to scrub clean. Chickens like to be alone when they lay eggs, so it's easy to coax them into using the box. Line it with straw or pine pet bedding to make it inviting. Buy fake stone or ceramic eggs at the feed store and put them in the nest to encourage egg laying and to discourage egg pecking. Replace the straw or pine shavings in the nest frequently to keep the eggs clean and the hens coming back to the box. Count on one box for every three or four hens.

Freshly laid eggs are covered with bloom, an antibacterial coating. Bloom retards spoiling, keeps eggs from drying out, and prevents bacteria from getting in. Avoid washing the eggs if you can. If you do find dirt or chicken poop on them, gently wipe them clean with a damp towel. I store fresh eggs at room temperature and move them to the refrigerator if I don't use them within a few days. Refrigerated eggs will keep for about a month.

molting, brooding, and pecking

At times your chickens will behave in ways that will make you worry. I remember when one of my first hens looked just terrible, almost bare of feathers. I was so sure that she had a terminal infectious disease that I was thinking of ways to euthanize her so she wouldn't infect the flock. I was spared the embarrassment of taking her to the vet when I discovered that she was molting. A six-week process of loss and regrowth of feathers, molting happens annually after a chicken is a year old. It is more noticeable in some chickens than others. When hens are molting, they don't lay eggs.

A hen that sits on the egg nest all day can also cause worry. Seemingly at random, a nurturing instinct will overcome a hen and she will "go broody" and think she is incubating eggs. She will peck at you when you try to remove the eggs beneath her. Just keep nudging her off the nest and she will eventually forget about mothering.

If it seems like one of your chickens is being picked on, that's because she probably is. Chickens establish a pecking order and the one at the bottom is sometimes bullied. If a hen is being attacked, separate it from the rest of the flock for a brief spell. Chickens are very forgetful, so when you reintroduce the bird after an hour or so, they may pay her no mind at all.

This recipe uses a ton of cherry tomatoes and a half dozen eggs, so it's a super delicious way to cook up a surplus. Enjoy the frittata warm, at room temperature, or even cold, for breakfast, lunch, or with crusty bread and a green salad (page 33) for a simple dinner. I like to use thyme here, but basil or tarragon would be great too.

Preheat the oven to 450°F (230°C). In a bowl, whisk together the eggs and salt until well blended. Stir in both cheeses.

In a heavy, 9-inch (23-cm) frying pan over medium-high heat, warm the olive oil. Add the cherry tomatoes and cook, moving the pan back and forth over the burner occasionally, until the tomatoes begin to brown in spots, about 1 minute. Add the garlic and thyme and continue cooking until the tomatoes are tender and have burst, about 3 minutes.

Reduce the heat to low and shake the pan to distribute the tomatoes evenly over the bottom. Pour the egg mixture over the tomatoes and cook until the egg mixture is set at the edges, about 3 minutes. Using a heat-resistant rubber spatula, and working around the edge of the pan, gently separate the edge of the cooked eggs from the edge of the pan, allowing the uncooked portion to flow underneath. Carefully smooth the top with the spatula. When the eggs are softly set, after about 3 minutes, transfer the pan to the oven and bake until frittata is just set in the center, about 7 minutes.

Remove from the oven and let cool slightly, then sprinkle with additional thyme. Cut into wedges and serve warm or at room temperature. Or cover and refrigerate for up to 1 day and serve cold.

cherry tomato frittata with fresh thyme

large eggs, 6

kosher salt, ½ tsp

mozzarella cheese, ½ cup (2 oz/60 g) shredded

Parmesan cheese, ½ cup (2 oz/60 g) grated

extra-virgin olive oil, 1 tbsp

cherry tomatoes, ¾ lb (375 g), stemmed

garlic, 2 cloves, minced

fresh thyme leaves, 1 tbsp chopped, plus more for garnish

salad with poached egg, black pepper croutons & bacon

applewood-smoked bacon, 6 oz (185 g), cut into ¾-inch (2-cm) pieces

crustless country or sourdough bread cubes, 2 cups (4 oz/125 g), cut into ½-inch (12-mm) cubes

kosher salt and freshly ground pepper

shallot, ¼ cup (1 oz/30 g) sliced

red wine vinegar, 1 tbsp

Dijon mustard, ½ tsp

extra-virgin olive oil, 1 tbsp

salad greens, 4 cups (4 oz/125 g)

large eggs, 2

distilled white vinegar, 1 tbsp

MAKES 2 SERVINGS

When baby frisée lettuce is tossed with bacon and a shallot vinaigrette, then topped with a poached egg and croutons, it becomes the French favorite—salade lyonnaise. I don't often have frisée growing in my plot, but that doesn't stop me from enjoying one of my all-time favorite salads. Any flavorful green works well here—spinach, arugula, or escarole.

In a large frying pan over medium heat, fry the bacon until crisp and browned, about 6 minutes. Transfer the bacon to a small bowl. Pour off all but 1 tbsp of the bacon drippings into a small bowl and set aside. Return the pan to medium-low heat, add the bread cubes, and season generously with pepper. Cook, stirring frequently, until golden brown and toasted on all sides yet still chewy, about 10 minutes. Pour into a bowl and let cool.

Return the pan to medium heat and add 1½ tsp of the reserved drippings. Add the shallot and sauté just until tender, about 4 minutes. Add 1 tbsp water and deglaze the pan, stirring to scrape up any browned bits on the pan bottom. Transfer the shallot mixture to a small bowl. Add the red wine vinegar and mustard to the shallots, stir well, and let cool to room temperature. Whisk in the olive oil and season with salt and pepper.

Place the greens in a bowl, drizzle with the dressing, and toss to coat. Divide the salad between 2 plates, and sprinkle with the bacon pieces and croutons, dividing evenly.

In a saucepan, combine 4 cups (32 fl oz/1 l) water and the white vinegar and bring to a boil. Reduce the heat to medium-low to keep the water at a simmer. Crack an egg into a small bowl, then slip the egg from the bowl into the water. Repeat with the second egg. Use a large spoon to spoon the egg white back toward the center of the egg. Simmer gently until the egg white is opaque, 3–4 minutes. Using a slotted spoon, lift the egg out of the water, carefully blot the bottom of the spoon on paper towels to remove the excess water, then top each salad with an egg. Serve.

orecchiete carbonara with fava beans

kosher salt and freshly ground pepper

fava beans, 1 lb (500 g), shelled

applewood-smoked bacon, ¼ lb (125 g), diced

leeks, 2, white and pale green parts, thinly sliced

orecchiete, 10 oz (315 g)

large eggs, 2, at room temperature

Parmesan cheese, ½ cup (2 oz/ 60 g) grated, plus more for serving

fresh flat-leaf parsley leaves, 1 tbsp chopped

MAKES 4 SERVINGS

Leeks and fava beans add a fresh spring touch to this classic Roman egg-and-bacon pasta. The popular Pugliese pasta known as orecchiete, or "little ears," cups the sauce and the leek and bacon bits nicely.

Bring a saucepan three-fourths full of salted water to a boil. Add the fava beans and boil until the skins begin to blister, about 2 minutes. Drain the beans, let cool until they can be handled, and then slip off the skins.

In a large, heavy frying pan over medium heat, fry the bacon until crisp, about 8 minutes. Using a slotted spoon, transfer the bacon to paper towels to drain. Pour off all but 2 tbsp of the bacon drippings from the pan and return the pan to medium heat. Add the leeks and sauté until tender, about 4 minutes. Stir in the fava beans. Set aside and keep warm.

Meanwhile, cook the pasta. Bring a large pot of water to a rapid boil and salt generously. Add the pasta, stir well, and cook until al dente, about 10 minutes or according to package directions. Drain the pasta, reserving about ½ cup (4 fl oz/120 ml) of the cooking water.

Working quickly, in a bowl, whisk together the eggs, Parmesan, a generous pinch of salt, and a grind or two of pepper. Gradually whisk in ¼ cup (2 fl oz/60 ml) of the cooking water. Return the frying pan containing the leek mixture to medium heat, add the pasta, and stir to heat briefly. Remove from the heat, pour the egg mixture over the pasta, and stir until the pasta is just creamy, about 2 minutes. If the pasta is runny rather than creamy, return the pan to very low heat and stir constantly. (Be careful that the eggs don't curdle.) Add some of the remaining ¼ cup (2 fl oz/ 60 ml) cooking water if needed to moisten. Stir in the bacon and parsley.

Divide the pasta among warmed shallow bowls and serve. Pass additional cheese at the table.

quiche with spinach, feta & herbs

In the spring, when I am flush with eggs and spinach, I make this garden-inspired quiche. Be sure to make the pastry the night before you want to serve the quiche so it can rest overnight, which keeps the crust from shrinking when baked.

On a lightly floured work surface, roll out the dough into a 12-inch (30-cm) round. Transfer the round to a 9½-inch (24-cm) tart pan with 1¼-inch (3-cm) sides and a removable bottom, pressing it gently onto the bottom and sides. Trim the crust so that there is a ½-inch (12-mm) overhang. Fold the overhang inward and press the pastry onto the sides of the pan so it extends ¼ inch (6 mm) higher than the rim. Refrigerate the crust overnight.

Position a rack in the lower third of the oven and preheat to 450°F (230°C). Meanwhile, pierce the bottom of the crust with a fork and freeze for about 10 minutes. Line the crust with parchment paper and fill with pastry weights or dried beans. Bake until the pastry is golden at the edges, about 10 minutes. Remove from the oven, and remove the weights and parchment. Return the crust to the oven to bake until the bottom is golden, about 5 minutes longer. Let cool on a wire rack. Reduce the heat to 325°F (165°C).

Meanwhile, bring water to a boil in the bottom of a steamer. Place the spinach on the steamer rack, cover, and steam until wilted and tender, about 2 minutes. Lift out the rack and rinse the spinach briefly under running cold water until cool. Squeeze the spinach to remove excess moisture, then chop coarsely.

Sprinkle half of the feta over the bottom of the cooled crust. Top with half each of the spinach, green onions, and herbs. Top with the remaining feta, spinach, green onions, and herbs. Season with pepper. In a bowl, whisk together the eggs, milk, cream, and salt until well blended. Pour over the filling in the crust.

Bake until the filling is set in the center when the quiche is jiggled slightly, about 45 minutes. Let cool on a wire rack until warm, then cut into wedges to serve.

savory pastry dough (page 215)

spinach leaves, 10 cups (about 10 oz/315 g)

feta cheese, 6 oz (185 g), crumbled

green onions, 3, finely chopped

mixed fresh herbs such as mint, dill, and flat-leaf parsley, ⅓ cup (½ oz/15 g) minced

freshly ground pepper

large eggs, 6

whole milk, ¾ cup (6 fl oz/180 ml)

heavy cream, ½ cup (4 fl oz/125 ml)

kosher salt, ¼ tsp

egg salad sandwiches with chopped watercress

large eggs, 7

sour cream, ¼ cup (2 oz/60 g)

mayonnaise, 3 tbsp

whole-grain mustard, 3 tbsp

watercress leaves, ⅓ cup (½ oz/15 g) chopped, plus 1 cup (1 oz/30 g) sprigs

fresh chives, ¼ cup (⅓ oz/10 g) snipped

fresh garlic chives, 1 tbsp snipped (optional)

kosher salt and freshly ground pepper

whole-grain bread, 8 slices

MAKES 4 SERVINGS

I love the combination of rich creamy egg salad and peppery fresh watercress with plenty of chives. For dainty tea sandwiches, use a good-quality white bread, cut off the crusts, and cut the sandwiches into finger-size pieces.

To hard-boil the eggs, place them in a saucepan just large enough to hold them and add cold water to cover by 1 inch (2.5 cm). Bring just to a boil over high heat, then remove the pan from the heat and cover. Let stand for 15 minutes. Drain the eggs, then transfer to a bowl of ice water and let cool completely.

Peel the eggs and separate the yolks and whites. Crumble the egg yolks into a bowl. Finely chop the egg whites and add to the egg yolks. Add the sour cream, mayonnaise, and mustard and stir until well blended. Mix in the chopped watercress and both types of chives. Season with salt and pepper. (The egg salad can be covered and refrigerated for up to 2 days.)

Divide the egg salad among 4 slices of bread. Top each with watercress sprigs, dividing evenly, then top with the remaining bread slices. Cut each sandwich in half and serve.

soft scrambled eggs with ricotta & herbs

large eggs, 4

fresh chives, 2 tbsp snipped

mixed fresh herbs of choice, 1 tbsp minced

kosher salt and freshly ground pepper

unsalted butter, 1 tbsp

ricotta cheese, ⅓ cup (3 oz/90 g)

whole-grain bread, 4 slices, lightly toasted and buttered

MAKES 2 SERVINGS

You can use any combination of delicate herbs in these velvety scrambled eggs, including basil, tarragon, dill, cilantro, and even mint. A marbling of fresh ricotta cheese brings out the creaminess of the eggs in this decadent but quick-to-prepare dish.

In a bowl, whisk together the eggs, 1 tbsp of the chives, and the mixed herbs until well blended. Season lightly with salt.

In a heavy, well-seasoned or nonstick frying pan over medium heat, melt the butter. When the foam subsides, add the egg mixture and cook, stirring constantly with a heat-resistant spatula, until the eggs are almost cooked but are still slightly runny in parts, 1–2 minutes. Remove the pan from the heat. Stir in the ricotta, but do not blend it in fully. Small clumps of the cheese should be visible.

Arrange 2 toasts on each plate. Divide the egg mixture evenly between the plates, spooning it on top of the toasts. Sprinkle each serving with salt and a grind or two pepper. Garnish with the remaining 1 tbsp chives, dividing it evenly, and serve.

zabaglione with muscat & honey

sugar, 3 tbsp

orange zest, ½ tsp grated

large egg yolks, 6

white muscat wine,
¾ cup (6 fl oz/180 ml)

honey, 2 tbsp

You will need stamina to make this delicate Italian custard, as the eggs and wine must be steadily whisked over simmering water until thick and foamy. The zabaglione can be served warm with biscotti on the side, or it can be served chilled, in small bowls topped with fresh fruit.

Put the sugar and orange zest into a large metal bowl, and rub them together between your fingertips to release the essential oils in the zest. Add the egg yolks and whisk until well blended. Gradually whisk in the wine and honey.

Bring a saucepan half filled with water to a simmer. Set the bowl holding the egg yolk mixture over (not touching) the water. Whisk the mixture until it is thick and foamy and an instant-read thermometer inserted into it registers 160°F (40°C), about 4 minutes.

Spoon the zabaglione into individual dishes and either serve right away, or let cool, cover, and refrigerate before serving.

caramel egg custard

sugar, 1¾ cups (14 oz/440 g)

large whole eggs, 5

large egg yolks, 5

kosher salt, ¼ tsp

whole milk, 4 cups (32 fl oz/1 l)

vanilla bean, 1, split lengthwise

Here is my version of the classic crème caramel of the French kitchen. It is not over-the-top rich like crème brûlée, but it still makes an impact with its silky texture and the flavors of caramel, vanilla, and fresh eggs. I also like to make individual portions by dividing the caramel and egg custard evenly between 8 small ramekins; the baking time might be reduced slightly, so start checking the custards after 30 minutes.

Preheat the oven to 400°F (200°C). In a heavy saucepan over medium heat, stir together 1 cup (8 oz/250 g) of the sugar and ¼ cup (2 fl oz/60 ml) water until the sugar dissolves. Raise the heat to high, bring to a boil, and boil without stirring, swirling the pan occasionally, until the sugar melts and turns a deep nut brown, about 6 minutes. If necessary, brush down the sides of the pan with a wet pastry brush to prevent crystals from forming. When the caramel is ready, immediately pour it into an 8-inch (20-cm) soufflé dish and swirl the dish carefully to coat the bottom and about 2 inches (5 cm) up the sides with the caramel. Set the dish aside, and reserve the pan (do not wash).

In a bowl, whisk together the whole eggs, egg yolks, the remaining ¾ cup (6 oz/190 g) sugar, and the salt until well blended. Add the milk and vanilla bean to the pan used for the caramel, place over medium heat, and bring almost to a simmer, whisking occasionally. Remove from the heat and gradually whisk the hot milk into the egg mixture. Strain the custard through a fine-mesh sieve into the caramel-lined soufflé dish.

Place the dish in a baking pan, fill the pan with hot water to reach halfway up the sides of the soufflé dish, and cover the soufflé dish with aluminum foil. Bake until the custard is set in the center and a knife inserted into the center comes out clean, about 45 minutes.

Remove the pan from the oven, and remove the soufflé dish from the water. Let the custard cool completely. (The cooled custard can be covered and refrigerated for up to 3 days.) To serve, run a small, sharp knife around the inside edge of the dish to release the custard. Invert a rimmed platter on top of the soufflé dish and invert the dish and platter together. Lift off the soufflé dish and serve.

AN INTRODUCTION TO BEES

Honeybees are amazing. While these small flying insects go about their important business of making flowers turn into fruits, they store food in the form of delicious honey. Fortunately, they produce such a large surplus of the sweet, sticky fluid that they have enough to sustain themselves and share with us. The rewards of keeping bees are plenty. They help your garden—vegetables, fruits, flowers— thrive and will stock your pantry with delicious, nutritious honey for everything from muffins to mousse.

beehives

Beekeeping can happen just about anywhere: in the country, in a suburban garden, or even in a crowded city. A beehive can be installed by a back door, in a field or vacant lot, or on a downtown rooftop. Bees don't require a lot of space, nor do you need to own fields of flowers. They will travel for miles to forage for what they need, and all flowers and fruit trees are fair game. When you consider that there is a locally adapted bee that thrives from the equator to as far north as Alaska, you know that beekeeping is a truly universal endeavor.

picking the ideal spot

Even though you can "keep" bees anywhere, you need to consider a few things when deciding where to put your hive. First, you'll want to position it so that it faces southeast. That way, the bees will get a sunny start to the day and will begin to forage early. Bees will do best in an area with dry, firm ground and dappled light. Too much sun and they will be distressed during hot summer days. Too much shade and they will be cold, damp, and listless. Choose an airy place, free from damp gullies or windy peaks. A fence or hedge makes an excellent windbreak. Be sure the area is level from side to side and the hive can be canted slightly toward the front, so that rain won't run into it.

Lastly, you want your beehive to be accessible to you. Place it where you can visit easily and work comfortably with the bees, especially during honey harvesting.

forage

Forage—flowering plants—is the lifeblood of bees. Without forage, there is no nectar, no pollen, and therefore no honey. And, of course, it is best if the forage is untreated. Colony collapse disorder (the sudden disappearance of worker bees) has been largely attributed to the poisoning of commercial bees by chemical pesticides applied to the crops they pollinate. It comes as no surprise that small-scale urban beekeeping is relatively healthy because of plentiful untreated forage. Blooming plants are essential to the hive being a happy home, but because bees can fly as far as three miles from their hive to find nectar and pollen, they are sure to find forage.

water

A clean source of water is important for hive success. You don't want your bees to expend energy just looking for a drink, so the water should be close to the hive. A natural source is great, but bees are happy to hydrate with a watering device used for pets or chickens. At my house, the water source resembles a narrow, meandering creek that cascades into a small plant-filled fishpond. Wild bees have always enjoyed drinking from the pond and cooling off on the mossy stones, and now my bees do too. The pond is on the patio and my family and I enjoy sitting there on summer evenings watching the bees as they watch us.

setting up your hive structure

With a location settled, your next task is to select a hive structure. The box hive most people are familiar with is called the Langstroth hive, named for the nineteenth-century Pennsylvania reverend who

BEEKEEPING TOOLS

In addition to the hive itself, you will need to invest in some equipment. A protective bee suit, a hat with a veil, a pair of sturdy gloves, a smoker, and a hive tool are musts. The smoker has a chamber for smoldering burlap or paper and a bellow. It is used to blow cool smoke in and around the beehive during inspection. The smoke makes the bees think a forest fire is near. They panic and promptly gorge on honey, which makes them slow and docile. The hive tool, which looks like a small crowbar, is great for removing honey and propolis (sealing wax made by bees), stuck lids, and frames. A soft-bristled bee brush is also handy for gently sweeping away bees as you work.

invented it. Langstroth hives are stacked boxes that contain eight to ten frames on which the bees make or draw comb. The bottom box has an opening where the bees enter and exit. The benefit of this hive style is that most of the reproduction activity goes on in the lower "story," or box, and the honey is made and stored in the upper level, called the honey super, making harvesttime easier for the beekeeper.

A second hive style is the top bar, which is an inexpensive alternative to the Langstroth and is popular in developing countries and among many hobbyists elsewhere. The top bar hive consists of the body, a set of wooden bars set on top of the body, and a cover. Bees reproduce and make honey all in the same frame. At harvesttime, the beekeeper must be very careful not to damage developing bees as he or she lifts out the combs. Also, during peak production, the bees must be monitored to make sure that they don't draw comb between the frames, which can make it almost impossible to harvest honey or inspect the bees without harming the hive.

acquiring bees

With your beehive in place, it would be wonderful if bees just simply moved in. Although this is possible, it's not likely. You could capture a swarm in the wild or even mail-order "package" bees, but the best way to acquire bees is to purchase a "nuc" hive from a local apiarist. A nuc (short for nucleus) is basically a small, complete hive that includes a few frames of comb, a queen, bees, brood, and eggs. To find a good source for a nuc hive, contact a local beekeeping club or speak to the folks who sell honey at your local farmers' market.

I purchased a nuc from a local beekeeper. It was fun for the family to pile into the car and drive out to the foothills, where the beekeeper had a few hives. We brought our bottom box and swapped some empty frames for some bee-coated brood comb. Protected by our suits and accompanied by an expert beekeeper, we were able to identify worker bees, capped brood, eggs, drones, and the magnificent queen! We covered the box with a tarp to keep the bees from escaping and drove them to their new home. To get them accustomed to their new home, we fed the bees with a syrup made from equal parts water and sugar, dispensed from an attachable bee feeder, and pollen patties purchased at the beekeeping supply store.

inspecting your hive

You can read books or attend seminars about bees, surf beekeeping websites, and join a beekeepers' club, but the best way to learn about bees is to observe them, both outside and inside the hive. Outside the hive in early spring, you can look for test flights from newly emerged bees or even the mating flight of a virgin queen. Later in the season, you can

watch for bees returning with full pollen sacs. If there's plenty of bee traffic, it's likely that things are good within the hive, but it's important to check inside too.

To inspect your hive, suit up, calm down, and light your smoker. Blow smoke around the hive and very carefully into its entrance, making sure that the smoke is cool. Carefully remove the top lid without banging or jostling the hive, as sudden movement or noise will anger the bees. Drape the open hive with a few more puffs of smoke. If you have a relatively new hive, there might not be much going on in the honey super, but go ahead and remove a few frames. Your hope is that the bees have begun to make and store honey there. Carefully remove the super to reveal the bottom box. This is where the action is. Here you want to see stored pollen, freshly emerging bees, and capped brood. You also want to inspect for eggs to make sure that your queen is healthy and active, though this is easier said than done. Remove the frame at the end of the box and carefully lean it against the side of the hive. Pull frames gently toward the open space. Remove a frame near the center, being careful not to crush any bees, especially the queen. Hold the frame up to the light and look for tiny rice grain–like eggs (if you normally wear reading glasses, put them on). If you see eggs, then you've hit pay dirt and you can reassemble and close up the hive.

harvesting honey

Most hobby apiarists harvest their honey treasure by either specializing in cut-comb honey or using a low-tech crush-and-strain technique to yield jars of clear, fluid golden honey.

Cut-comb is honey-filled comb that is cut from the frame and transferred to a shallow jar or crock. The honey is then scraped from the cells of the comb as needed. Because the honey is not aerated, its flavor is considered the purest. To employ the crush-and-strain method, after you remove the honeycomb-filled frames from the hive, cut the comb from the frame, leaving about 1 inch (2.5 cm) of comb along the top so that your bees can draw more comb. Transfer the comb to a bucket and crush it with a large knife. Drill a few holes into the bottom of another large bucket and line it with a paint strainer. Set this bucket atop a third bucket and then pour the crushed comb and its honey into the improvised honey strainer. At this point, you'll need to wait a few days for the honey to strain into the bucket.

Fall and winter are slow times for bees and beekeepers. When you harvest honey, be sure to leave about four full frames of honey for your bees to feed on during the winter. If you keep bees in a cold climate, you can attach a feeder to your hive and fill it with sugar syrup made from the same formula you used when you first brought the bees home.

LEGAL ISSUES

Before you decide to keep bees, look into local laws and ordinances and make sure that your neighbors are supportive. If they aren't at first, they can often be sweetened with a little honey. Also, if you are allergic to bees, bee stings can be lethal. As bee stings are nearly unavoidable for beekeepers, you need to determine if you or any of your family members are allergic. If you discover one of you is at risk, participate in beekeeping by purchasing local honey and supporting the efforts of local beekeepers who practice natural beekeeping.

goat cheese toasts with walnuts, honey & thyme

whole-grain bread, 4 slices, each about 2½ by 5 inches (6 by 13 cm), lightly toasted

fresh goat cheese, 3 oz (90 g), at room temperature

walnuts, ¼ cup (1 oz/30 g) coarsely chopped

roasted walnut oil, 1 tsp

sea salt and freshly cracked black pepper

honey, for drizzling

fresh thyme leaves, ½ tsp

MAKES 2–4 SERVINGS

Dripping with honey and sprinkled with fresh thyme, cracked pepper, and sea salt, these warm, crunchy toasts make a delicious breakfast, after-school treat, or lunch when matched with a handful of salad greens. I'm always amazed how something so simple, and a tad messy, can be so unbelievably good.

Preheat the oven or toaster oven to 375°F (190°C). Arrange the toasts on a small rimmed baking sheet. Spread the toast slices evenly with the goat cheese, and sprinkle with the walnuts, dividing them evenly. Drizzle ¼ tsp of the walnut oil over each toast. Bake until the walnuts are toasted and the cheese is warm, about 5 minutes.

Transfer the toasts to plates and season with salt and pepper. Drizzle each toast with honey, then sprinkle with the thyme leaves and serve.

honey butter

salted butter, 4 tbsp (2 oz/60 g), at room temperature

honey, ½ cup (6 oz/185 g)

MAKES 6 SERVINGS

Recipes with only two components rely on using the best ingredients you can get, and when I use honey from my bees and locally made organic butter—I know I'm doing just that. This is heavenly spread on slices of freshly baked whole-wheat bread, fluffy biscuits, or warm toast.

In a small bowl, stir the butter until it is creamy. Gradually add the honey, stirring until creamy and emulsified. Use right away or store.

To store, spoon it onto the center of a sheet of waxed paper, then roll the butter in the paper, forming a log. Twist the ends to seal the log and refrigerate for up to 1 month. Cut the log into rounds to serve.

At first this might seem an odd combo, but it's really quite divine—especially if, like me, you love salty and sweet in one bite. You can begin or end a meal with this Greek-inspired small plate. Serve it with olives and nuts as a starter, or figs and grapes for dessert.

Preheat the oven to 400°F (200°C). Brush a shallow 10-inch (25-cm) oval gratin dish with olive oil.

Cut the feta into sticks. Arrange the sticks in the gratin dish, spacing them evenly. Brush the feta with olive oil and sprinkle with the aniseeds.

Bake until the feta is just browned at the edges, about 10 minutes. Drizzle the feta with the honey and sprinkle with the mint. Serve the feta hot with the baguette slices.

honey-drizzled baked feta with anise & mint

extra-virgin olive oil, for brushing

feta cheese, ½ lb (250 g)

aniseeds, 1 tsp

honey, 2 tbsp

fresh mint leaves, 1½ tbsp chopped

baguette slices, for serving

Pair this tangy yogurt panna cotta with honey-sweetened fruit: strawberries in spring, raspberries in summer, figs in fall, and oranges in winter. I like to serve it in a deep ceramic bowl made by a friend of mine, but it can also be made in individual bowls.

In a small bowl, sprinkle the gelatin over the milk and let stand until the gelatin softens, about 10 minutes.

Meanwhile, in a bowl, stir together ½ cup (4 fl oz/125 ml) of the cream and the yogurt until well blended. In a heavy saucepan over medium heat, combine the remaining ½ cup cream and the honey and bring to a simmer. Remove from the heat, add the gelatin mixture, and stir until the gelatin dissolves. Stir the gelatin mixture into the yogurt mixture.

Divide the mixture among small glasses or bowls. Cover and refrigerate until set, at least 2 hours or up to 2 days. Serve chilled.

honey & yogurt panna cotta

unflavored gelatin, 1 tsp

whole milk, ½ cup (4 fl oz/125 ml), cold

heavy cream, 1 cup (8 fl oz/250 ml)

plain yogurt, ½ cup (4 oz/125 g)

honey, ¼ cup (3 oz/90 g), plus more for serving

honey-nut raisin bran muffins

unsalted butter, ½ cup (4 oz/ 125 g), at room temperature, plus more for the muffin cups

honey, 1 cup (12 oz/375 g)

walnuts, 1½ cups (6 oz/185 g), toasted (page 217) and chopped

wheat bran, 1 cup (5 oz/155 g)

raisins, ⅔ cup (4 oz/125 g)

boiling water, 1 cup (8 fl oz/250 ml)

unbleached all-purpose flour, 1¼ cups (6½ oz/200 g)

whole-wheat flour, 1 cup (5 oz/155 g)

baking soda, 2 tsp

kosher salt, 1¾ tsp

sugar, ¾ cup (6 oz/185 g)

large eggs, 2

buttermilk, 1¾ cups (14 fl oz/430 ml)

MAKES 24 MUFFINS

When I was a little girl my mother would buy bran muffins at the bakery that were small, gooey, and baked with actual honey. Here I re-create the baked good of my youth—with a sticky honey-walnut glaze that tops the muffins when the tins are inverted.

Preheat the oven to 400°F (200°C). Brush 24 standard muffin cups generously with butter. Spoon ½ tsp of the honey onto the bottom of each muffin cup. Place 1 tbsp walnuts on top of the honey in each muffin cup.

In a heatproof bowl, combine the bran and raisins. Pour in the boiling water and mix well. In another bowl, whisk together both flours, the baking soda, and the salt. In a third bowl, using a handheld mixer on medium speed, beat together the butter and sugar until light and fluffy. Add the remaining ¾ cup (9 oz/280 g) honey and then the eggs, beating well after each addition. Mix in the bran mixture on low speed. Mix in half of the buttermilk, then the flour mixture. Add the remaining buttermilk, mixing just until combined.

Spoon the batter into the prepared muffin cups, dividing it evenly and filling each cup about three-fourths full. Bake until a toothpick inserted into the center of a muffin comes out clean, about 20 minutes.

Remove from the oven and let cool slightly in the pan. Run a small, sharp knife around the inside edge of each cup to loosen the muffin sides. Invert a rimmed baking sheet over one of the muffin tins, invert together, and lift off the muffin tin. Repeat with the second muffin tin and serve.

bittersweet chocolate—honey sauce

kosher salt, ¼ tsp

bittersweet chocolate, 8 oz (250 g), chopped

heavy cream, 2 tbsp

honey, 2 tbsp

MAKES ABOUT 1½ CUPS (12 FL OZ/375 ML)

Honey complements bittersweet chocolate in this intensely flavored sauce. I love to give jars of it as hostess or holiday gifts, to be spooned over ice cream or fruit.

In a small, heavy saucepan over medium-high heat, combine ½ cup (4 fl oz/125 ml) water and the salt and bring to a simmer. Remove from the heat, add the chocolate, and whisk until the chocolate melts. Add the cream and honey and whisk until the sauce is smooth.

Use right away, or transfer to a clean jar with a tight-fitting lid and refrigerate for up to 2 weeks. To serve, reheat gently in a microwave oven or in a small saucepan over low heat just until warm.

frozen honey cream

heavy cream, 1 cup (8 fl oz/250 ml), cold

honey, ¼ cup (3 oz/90 g), plus more for drizzling (optional)

large egg whites, 2

kosher salt, pinch

sugar, ¼ cup (2 oz/60 ml)

fresh lavender blossoms, for garnish (optional)

MAKES 6–8 SERVINGS

Whenever I serve this luscious dessert to friends, they are amazed that you don't need an ice cream maker to achieve the creamy texture. Honey has a low freezing point, so even though this mousse is simply frozen in a tub, the texture is magical. Serve it on its own, with the chocolate sauce above, or with fruit.

In a bowl, using a handheld mixer, beat together the cream and honey on low speed until the honey dissolves. Increase the speed to high and whip until peaks form.

Rinse the beaters and dry well, then refit to the mixer. In a large bowl, using the mixer on high speed, beat together the egg whites and salt until foamy. Gradually add the sugar and whip until medium peaks form. Using a rubber spatula, fold the egg whites gently but thoroughly into the whipped cream mixture. Transfer the mousse to a 3-cup (24–fl oz/750-ml) container and freeze overnight.

Spoon the mousse into shallow serving dishes and drizzle with a small amount of additional honey, if desired. If you like, sprinkle each portion with lavender blossoms just before serving.

BASIC RECIPES

pizza dough

lukewarm water, 1 cup (8 fl oz/250 ml)

active dry yeast, 1½ tsp

unbleached all-purpose flour, 2¾ cups (14 oz/440 g),
plus more for dusting

vital wheat gluten (pure gluten flour) or
bread flour, 3 tbsp

kosher salt, 1½ tsp

extra-virgin olive oil, 2 tbsp, plus more for brushing

In a 2-cup (16–fl oz/500-ml) measuring pitcher, whisk
together the water and yeast. Let stand for 5 minutes.

In a food processor, combine the flour, the wheat
gluten, and the salt and process to mix. Whisk the
olive oil into the yeast mixture. With the processor
running, add the yeast mixture and process until
the dough comes together and forms a ball, about
1 minute. (If the dough does not form a ball, add
water by tablespoonfuls until it comes together.)

Turn the dough out onto a lightly floured work
surface and knead briefly until smooth. Brush a large
bowl with olive oil. Shape the dough into a ball, place
it in the bowl, and turn the dough to coat it with oil.
Cover the bowl with a kitchen towel and let stand
until doubled in volume, about 1½ hours.

Punch down the dough and divide in half. Use at
once, or shape each half into a ball, place each ball
in a resealable plastic bag, and refrigerate for up to
2 days or freeze for up to 1 month.

Let the refrigerated dough stand for 1 hour and the
frozen dough thaw for 4 hours at room temperature
before using.

MAKES ABOUT 1½ LB (680 G) DOUGH OR ENOUGH FOR 2 PIZZAS

savory pastry dough

unbleached all-purpose flour, 1½ cups (7½ oz/235 g)

kosher salt, ½ tsp

cold unsalted butter, ⅔ cup (5 oz/155 g),
cut into small pieces

ice-cold water, 4–5 tbsp (2–2½ fl oz/60–75 ml)

In a food processor, combine the flour and kosher
salt and process to mix. Scatter the butter over the
flour mixture and pulse until the mixture resembles
coarse cornmeal. With the processor running, add
4 tbsp of the water and process just until moist clumps
form. If the dough is too dry to clump, add the
remaining 1 tbsp water and pulse just until combined.

Turn the dough out onto a lightly floured work
surface and gather it into a ball. Flatten the ball into
a disk. Wrap in plastic wrap and refrigerate for at
least 20 minutes before using.

MAKES ENOUGH DOUGH FOR ONE 9- TO 10-INCH (23–25-CM) CRUST

sweet pastry dough

unbleached all-purpose flour, 1½ cups (7½ oz/235 g)

sugar, ¼ cup (2 oz/60 g)

kosher salt, ½ tsp

unsalted butter, ½ cup plus 2 tbsp (5 oz/155 g), melted
and cooled slightly, plus butter for pan(s)

In a medium bowl, whisk together the flour, sugar,
and salt until blended. Add the butter and stir with
a fork until moist clumps form. Gently gather the
dough into a ball.

If pre-baking tartlet shells, preheat the oven to 375°F
(190°C). Butter four 4-inch (10-inch) tartlet pans with
1-inch (2.5-cm) sides and removable bottoms. Cut
the dough into 4 equal portions. Press each portion

evenly over the bottom and up the sides of a tartlet pan. Bake until golden brown, about 17 minutes. Let cool completely on a wire rack before filling.

If pre-baking a tart or pie shell, preheat the oven to 375°F (190°C). Butter a 9-inch (23-cm) tart pan with a removable bottom or a 9-inch (23-cm) pie dish. Press the dough evenly over the bottom and sides of the pan or dish, forming an attractive rim if making a pie shell. Bake until golden brown, about 17 minutes. Let cool completely on a wire rack before filling.

MAKES FOUR 4-INCH (10-CM) TARTLET SHELLS OR
ONE 9-INCH (23-CM) PIE OR TART SHELL

lemon-herb mayonnaise

large egg yolk, 1

Dijon mustard, 1 tbsp

garlic, 1 clove, pressed

canola oil, 3 tbsp

extra-virgin olive oil, 3 tbsp

fresh lemon juice, 2 tsp

lemon zest, 1 tsp finely grated

kosher salt and freshly ground pepper

fresh chives, 1 tbsp snipped

fresh flat-leaf parsley, 1 tbsp minced

In a small, deep bowl, vigorously whisk together the egg yolk, mustard, and garlic until blended. Combine the oils in a small measuring pitcher. Drizzle about 2 tsp of the oil mixture over the egg mixture and whisk vigorously for about 30 seconds to blend thoroughly. Repeat two more times, at which point the mixture should be emulsified. In a slow, steady stream, add the remaining oil mixture while whisking constantly. Continue to whisk until the mayonnaise thickens to a spreadable consistency. Whisk in the lemon juice and zest and season with salt and pepper. Stir in the herbs. Serve right away, or cover and refrigerate for up to 4 days.

MAKES ABOUT ½ CUP (4 FL OZ/125 ML)

creamy polenta

unsalted butter, 2 tbsp

kosher salt, 1 tsp

coarse-ground polenta or yellow cornmeal,
1 cup (7 oz/220 g)

Parmesan cheese, ½ cup (2 oz/ 60 g) grated

freshly ground pepper

In a heavy saucepan, bring 4 cups (32 fl oz/1 l) water, the butter, and the salt to a boil over high heat. Add the polenta in a thin, steady stream while whisking constantly. Reduce the heat to medium and continue to whisk for 1 minute. Reduce the heat to low, cover, and cook, stirring occasionally, until thick and creamy, about 40 minutes.

Remove from the heat, stir in the Parmesan, and season with pepper. Serve right away or cover tightly and leave at room temperature for up to 20 minutes before serving.

MAKES 4 SERVINGS

candied pecans

golden brown sugar, ¼ cup (2 oz/60 g) firmly packed

pecans halves, 1 cup (4 oz/125 g)

kosher salt

In a heavy, nonstick frying pan over medium heat, combine the brown sugar and 4 tsp water. Bring to a boil and cook until the mixture bubbles thickly, about 20 seconds. Add the pecans and cook, stirring occasionally, until the pecans are lightly toasted and coated with the syrup, about 4 minutes.

Transfer the pecans to a piece of parchment paper and sprinkle with salt. Using a fork, separate the pecans. Let cool completely.

Use right away, or store in an airtight jar at room temperature for up to 1 week.

MAKES 1 GENEROUS CUP (4½ OZ/140 G)

pastry cream

whole milk, 1 cup (8 fl oz/250 ml)

vanilla bean, ½, split lengthwise

large egg yolks, 3

sugar, ¼ cup (2 oz/60 g)

cornstarch, 1½ tbsp

In a heavy saucepan over medium heat, combine the milk and vanilla bean. Warm the mixture until small bubbles appear around the edge of the pan. Meanwhile, in a bowl, whisk together the egg yolks, sugar, and cornstarch until blended.

Gradually whisk the hot milk into the egg mixture. Return the mixture to the saucepan and whisk over medium heat until the mixture thickens and boils gently, about 1 minute.

Transfer to a small bowl, cover with plastic wrap, pressing it directly onto the surface to prevent a skin from forming, and refrigerate until well chilled, about 2 hours, before using.

MAKES ABOUT 1 CUP (8 FL OZ/250 ML)

vanilla whipped cream

heavy cream, 1 cup (8 fl oz/250 ml)

sugar, about 1 tbsp

pure vanilla extract, 1 tsp

In the bowl of a mixer fitted with the whisk, add the cream, sugar to taste, and vanilla. Beat on medium-high speed until medium peaks form. Don't overwhip the cream, or it will become stiff and grainy. Serve right away or cover with plastic wrap and serve within 2 hours; fluff the whipped cream with a whisk before serving.

MAKES ABOUT 2 CUPS (16 FL OZ/500 ML)

segmenting citrus

Using a serrated knife, cut a slice off the top and bottom of a grapefruit, orange, or other citrus fruit to expose the flesh. Stand the fruit upright and cut off the peel and pith, slicing downward and following the contour of the fruit. Working over a bowl, make a cut on both sides of each segment to release it from the membrane, letting the segment and any juice drop into the bowl. Pour off the juice from the bowl into a small bowl, then squeeze the juice from the membrane into the small bowl.

toasting nuts & seeds

Be sure to toast nuts and seeds just before you are ready to use them. Preheat the oven to 350°F (180°C). Spread the nuts or seeds in a single layer on a small rimmed baking sheet and toast, stirring occasionally, until fragrant, 2–10 minutes for seeds and 5–15 minutes for nuts. The timing will vary depending on the type or size; check regularly to avoid burning.

toasting & skinning hazelnuts

Preheat the oven to 350°F (180°C). Spread the hazelnuts in a single layer in a small pan and toast until they are fragrant and taking on color, about 10 minutes. Pour the warm nuts into a coarse-textured kitchen towel and rub them vigorously between your palms to remove the skins. Don't worry if bits of skin remain.

INDEX

weldon**owen**

415 Jackson Street, Suite 200, San Francisco, CA 94111
www.weldonowen.com

KITCHEN GARDEN COOKBOOK
Conceived and produced by Weldon Owen, Inc.
Copyright © 2013 Weldon Owen, Inc.
and Williams-Sonoma, Inc.

All rights reserved, including the right of reproduction
in whole or in part in any form.

Printed in China by Toppan Leefung

First printed in 2013
10 9 8 7 6 5 4 3 2

Library of Congress Control Number: 2012954913

ISBN 13: 978-1-61628-557-9
ISBN 10: 1-61628-557-5

Weldon Owen is a division of
BONNIER

WELDON OWEN, INC.
CEO and President Terry Newell
VP, Sales and Marketing Amy Kaneko
Director of Finance Mark Perrigo

VP and Publisher Hannah Rahill
Executive Editor Kim Laidlaw

Creative Director Emma Boys
Art Directors Alexandra Zeigler and Kara Church
Associate Art Director Ashley Lima

Production Director Chris Hemesath
Production Manager Michelle Duggan

Photographer Ray Kachatorian
Food Stylist Jeanne Kelley
Prop Stylist Jennifer Barguiarena
Illustrations Salli Swindell

Additional photography by: Maren Caruso: pages 13
(lower left), 142, 153 (top right), 169 (top and bottom left);
Erin Kunkel: pages 2, 35, 42, 48, 85, 86, 115, 119 (top right),
122, 151, 185, 191, 214; Ashley Lima: pages 61 (bottom right),
77 (bottom right), 111 (top right), 119 (top left);
Kate Sears: page 56

ACKNOWLEDGMENTS

From Jeanne: Gratitude to my husband, Martin, for his gardening expertise; he is the true green thumb
in our yard. As always, my daughters, Celeste and Theresa, play a huge part in my cooking due to their
good appetites, keen palates, and mad dishwashing skills. Many thanks to the team at Weldon Owen
and Williams-Sonoma for appreciating the simple pleasures and goals of this book.

Weldon Owen wishes to thank the following people for their generous support in producing this book:
David Bornfriend, Lydia Burkhalter, Jane Tunks Demel, Max Gray, Melissa Kinnicutt, Erin Kunkel, Jeff Larsen,
Rachel Lopez Metzger, Francesca Parnham, Elizabeth Parson, Michael Turner, and Robyn Valarik.